"After 20 years as a professional in the animal world, I realized after reading the first few chapters of Saying Goodbye to the Pet You Love that I was privileged to be holding a practical yet humane resource, that not only legitimizes grieving the loss of a pet but helps people understand how to deal with the loss. It has something for every type of person who has been touched by such an event."

—Mark Goldstein, DVM, President, San Diego Humane Society and SPCA

"I wish that a book like this had been available to me when one of my rabbits died suddenly. Lorri Greene was of immense help to me at that time and I've been able to pass along much of her advice to others who have lost their pets. This book will be a wonderful resource for those of us who love our pets and need help coping with their inevitable passings."

—Amy Spintman, educator, House Rabbit Society (San Diego Chapter)

"Lorri Greene provides healing suggestions necessary to work into, through, and out of the deep and painful experiences of pet loss and recovery."

—Peter L. Poses, Ph.D., LMFT, and Ruth Gussman, DVM, Pet Loss Facilitators for The Human-Animal Bond Trust of Colorado (Hab/T)

SAYING
GOOD-BYE
TO THE
PET YOU
LOVE

**A COMPLETE RESOURCE
TO HELP YOU HEAL**

Lorri A. Greene, Ph.D. • Jacquelyn Landis

Foreword by Alan M. Beck, Sc.D.

New Harbinger Publications, Inc.

Publisher's Note

This publication is designed to provide accurate and authoritative information in regard to the subject matter covered. It is sold with the understanding that the publisher is not engaged in rendering psychological, financial, legal, or other professional services. If expert assistance or counseling is needed, the services of a competent professional should be sought.

Distributed in the U.S.A. by Publishers Group West; in Canada by Raincoast Books; in Great Britain by Hi Marketing, Ltd.; in South Africa by Real Books, Ltd.; in Australia by Boobook; and in New Zealand by Tandem Press.

Copyright © 2002 by Lorri A. Greene and Jacquelyn Landis
New Harbinger Publications, Inc.
5674 Shattuck Avenue
Oakland, CA 94609

Cover design by Amy Shoup
Cover image by Ryuichi Sato/Photonica
Edited by Kayla Sussell
Text design by Tracy Powell-Carlson

ISBN 1-57224-307-4 Paperback

Printed in the United States of America

New Harbinger Publications' Web site address: www.newharbinger.com

04   03   02

10   9   8   7   6   5   4   3   2   1

First printing

*Dedicated to anyone who has ever loved and lost
a companion animal.*

—Lorri Greene

To my mom and dad, whose love and support never waver.

—Jackie Landis

Contents

Acknowledgments

As with any work of this nature, there are many people who have contributed their time and expertise to this book. First and foremost, the authors wish to thank all of the people who have shared their stories of pet love and pet loss with Dr. Greene over the last twenty years. Without you, this book would not have been written. The authors are extremely grateful to Matthew McKay, Ph.D., editor in chief of New Harbinger Publications. It was Dr. McKay who thought this topic and this book would be a worthwhile addition to New Harbinger's publications. Jueli Gastwirth, senior acquisitions editor, provided support and kept the authors "on task" during the writing process. She made us smile on days when the road was difficult. Kayla Sussell, senior editor, made sure that our book met all of New Harbinger's high standards.

A very special thank-you to Dr. Alan Beck, who agreed to write the foreword. Dr. Beck has studied the human-animal bond his entire academic career and is considered one of the foremost scholars in this field. We are deeply grateful that he agreed to participate in this project.

His book, *Between Pets and People,* is considered "must" reading for anyone interested in this topic.

There are many people who gave freely of their time and talent to ensure the content of this book was accurate and informative. Thank you, Rose Brown, DVM, for your friendship and for providing veterinary information when needed. Along with Dr. Brown, several other wonderful veterinarians gave us useful ideas and made sure that the information presented to the reader was factual. These include: Sara Ford, DVM, Diplomate American College of Veterinary Internal Medicine, Gary Gallerstein, DVM, James Harris, DVM, Patrick Melese, MA, DVM, and Christine van Spronsen, DVM. The American Veterinary Medical Association, particularly Gail Golab, Ph.D., DVM., made available information that proved to be very useful. Amy Spintman, an educator for the House Rabbit Society, provided insight into the nature of rabbits. Any veterinary mistakes are errors by Dr. Greene.

We were blessed with wonderful research assistants. Summer Brooks was always there to help with researching anything we needed. She gave up many a Saturday helping facilitate pet-loss support groups. Sandy Reiten was also invaluable. Besides doing research, she made the original slides for the presentation that led to the invitation to write this book. George and Alice Guy made sure that we had all of the recent animal stories from every newspaper and magazine in the county of San Diego. They were a great help.

Every project needs a cheerleader. In our case it was Carol Gaffney, RVT. She pushed us on with her enthusiasm, perpetual smile, and monthly lunches. There were many people at the San Diego Humane Society who contributed to this work. Three individuals were particularly helpful: Dr. Mark Goldstein, president of the San Diego Humane Society; Ms. Susan Jenkins, who has always been there for us, and Captain Beauregard, who helped with the legal issues regarding pet guardianship.

Thanks to all of you who allowed us to share your stories of pain and loss. We hope that you will think it was worth it.

Dr. Greene's Personal Acknowledgments

I would like to take the opportunity to once more express my deep gratitude to all who have shared their stories of love and loss over the last twenty years. It has been my privilege to be a part of all of your lives. You were what kept me going when I didn't want to write another word.

I would also like to thank my husband, Dr. David Dozier, for being supportive and extra caring over these last months. His belief in my ability to co-write a book often exceeded my own. When I would get stuck he usually had a suggestion that would help me to continue writing. My daughters, Sara and Lara, were also there with a suggestion or a kind word when needed. When all else failed, I could count on their great sense of humor, reminding me to "breathe," rest, and eat; and their reminders that everything didn't have to be written in one day.

I would be remiss if I didn't thank my live-in feline friends, Tara and Bosco. Seventeen-year-old Tara has mastered the art of sunbathing from the upstairs patio. She has also taught me, since the time I rescued her from a Dumpster at three weeks of age, kindness, gentleness, and what unconditional love is really all about. Bosco, her ten-year-old sister, is a bit more lively. Her favorite hobby, next to eating, is "crashing" computers. However, she could not manage to deter my wonderful Macintosh iBook from its mission. Kudos to Steve Jobs and the people at Apple.

I would also like to thank my mother, Marty, my father, Larry, and my stepfather, Ray, for passing along to me their love of animals. My childhood was filled with both dogs and cats. I don't remember a time without them. My stepfather recently found a stray cat and took it home, hiding him under his jacket, just in case my mother didn't want an addition to the family. She did and they named it Happy. I think he's also very lucky! Thanks also to my brother, Bill, and sister-in-law, Karen, both for their enthusiasm for the book and their love of animals.

To my wonderful women friends who gave their love and support throughout the entire process. Special thanks to Dr. Denise Zimmerman, Dr. Debbie Zambianco, Dr. Carolyn Hudson, Dr. Rita Romero, Dr. Rose Brown, Jane Alshuler, and Carol Kelbride. I am fortunate to have you in my life.

Last, but certainly not least, thanks to my co-author, Jacquelyn Landis. She made this book readable as well as educational. Her Internet and computer skills were a tremendous asset, as was her ability to write a cohesive, yet interesting sentence. This book would have been tediously boring if written by me alone. In fact, it wouldn't have been written at all. Thanks, Jackie.

Jacquelyn Landis' Personal Acknowledgments

Everyone who has ever had a pet also has a story, and it is these stories that have both driven the need for this book and provided the empathetic basis for its readers. My fifteen-year-old cat, Kali, gives me daily reminders of why a book of this nature is so important. As I write this, I'm perched on a stool in front of my computer because Kali has, once again, decided to nap the day away in my chair. As she ages, I believe she deserves every comfort she can find, simply because she has brought so much joy to my life. Relinquishing my chair is a small price to pay.

Friends and family members will, no doubt, recognize their stories in these pages. I thank them not only for sharing their stories but also for sharing my love of animals. Most important, I thank Dr. Lorri Greene for her knowledge and experience and her desire to translate them into something of value for all animal lovers. I thank Lorri, too, for a wonderful collaborative experience. Her professionalism is exceeded only by her cheerful, optimistic personality. She has made this almost too easy.

Foreword

Bonding is the forming of close, specialized human relationships, such as the link between parent and child, husband and wife, friend and friend. Similar behaviors, often in similar settings, are seen in animals, especially among birds and mammals, and we often use the same term, "bonding," for them.

Domesticated animals, like our pets, are social species that exhibit social interactions and "bonding-like" behaviors among themselves, and perhaps that is why they are so able to socialize with us. Thus, "bonding-like" behaviors between people and their pets gave rise to the concept of the "human-animal bond." It is the general mutual exchange of reactions to similar cues, interpreted by people to mean the same emotional states, as if all were the same species. The power of bonding becomes most apparent, and most troubling, when one of the members of a bonded pair dies. This is true whether a person loses another person or a beloved pet.

Saying Good-bye to the Pet You Love does not immediately begin with the many issues involved in pet loss, like grief and guilt, or even with ways to help handle the tide of feelings; instead the book begins by discussing just why animals are so important to people in the first place. In the context of responses to pet loss, it is very helpful, indeed therapeutic, to understand why, and how, we relate to our loved companion animals. To that end, the book opens with a brief lesson in psychology and biology so we can better understand the role of companion animals in society today.

The authors alert us to those times when our animals may be especially important, perhaps even therapeutic; therefore, their loss may be especially traumatic. While psychologists and books about the human-animal bond often discuss this concept, it is often not discussed with people experiencing a loss. Being alerted to this concern, as with other issues related to pet loss, is very important for helping people in need. We must remember that pet loss occurs in lives that are already complex and, at times, challenging.

It is important to understand the nature of our attachment to animals, in other words why we feel as strongly about pets as we do. There is no best way to be bonded, only what is best for you. This level of bonding, or attachment, impacts on your grief response after a loss, and understanding that can only help in times of need after a loss. You are invited to assess your own level of attachment with an enclosed "take-home exam." Your final score is not a grade in the way a school exam is graded, but an instrument for you to better understand how animals fit into your own personal life. Of course, there are many permutations in the attachment equation, as people may have many pets, and family members may have different relationships with them. All of this deserves thought, thought best appreciated before a loss, and best used to understand your feelings afterwards.

This book is mainly about loss and grief. You will be invited to assess your own behaviors and responses to grief. In this way, you will gain an understanding that will help you better handle your loss with dignity and eventual recovery. *Saying Good-bye to the Pet You Love* is about how we feel about animals and how we feel about ourselves. With these insights, we can better enjoy our pets and continue, and thrive, even after they are gone.

—Alan M. Beck, Sc.D.
School of Veterinary Medicine
Purdue University

Author of *Between Pets and People:
The Importance of Animal Companionship*, 1996

March 18, 2002

Introduction

When I was a child, I was taught by my parents and teachers to read a book from the beginning until the end. You weren't supposed to skip around (and certainly not read the ending first!). I still read this way today. If I am reading a murder mystery, I don't skip to the last page to find out who did it. But this book is not intended to be read in that front-to-back way.

As I was writing, I occasionally had some difficulty deciding which verb tense to use. Many of you are reading this book because your pet has already died. But others may be preparing themselves for the day when their companion animal leaves this world. In trying to address situations that may not be universal for all readers, I decided to use the present tense for generalized statements and the past tense only where it is clearly appropriate.

Even though this book has two authors, we haven't shared every experience that we relate here. So when we begin a story or an insight with "I," please imagine that you are hearing Dr. Greene's voice.

How to Use This Book

If you choose to read this book from front to back, that's fine. However, if while browsing the table of contents, you find a particular chapter that appeals to you, perhaps because of what you are going through at the time, then read that chapter first. Each person is a unique individual and faces unique issues. This book is not intended to be a "one size fits all" treatise, although we have tried to cover as many issues as possible concerning pet loss and bereavement.

The same goes for the interactive exercises in the book. As a child, I was taught that everyone is supposed to write his or her ABCs the same way. But the activities, ideas, and advice provided here are simply suggestions that may help you get through your grief.

Many of the suggested activities will include some writing. Some of you may find that writing in a journal is helpful. Others may want to tape record their thoughts and feelings. Still others may just want to read and absorb the material. Do what is comfortable. This book was written for you.

Chapter 1

Making the Connection

The moral fiber of a nation can be judged by its treatment of animals.

—Mahatma Gandhi

In the Beginning

Have you ever wondered just how or when the connection between humankind and animals originated? On the surface, it seems an unlikely relationship to have evolved spontaneously. After all, people and animals are different species, and you don't often see sympathetic, bonded relationships between species.

But there's no denying that very close relationships do indeed develop between humans and their companion animals. Think about your own relationship with your pet. Do you talk to your cat? Do you call for your dog and greet it as soon as you come home from work? Do you buy special, organic lettuce for your turtle that you know it will like? These close, almost humanlike connections seem perfectly natural to us.

It wasn't always like that, however.

To best understand how animals and humans came to be friends, let's take a brief journey into the past and learn how man's (and woman's) best friend, whether dog, cat, bird, iguana, or whatever, took the first tentative steps into a trusting and loving relationship with human beings. By understanding the history of animals as pets, it will be easier for you to understand the modern-day attachments we have forged with them.

Dogs

Twelve thousand years ago, perhaps along the banks of what is now known as the Nile River in northern Africa, a remarkable event occurred. One lone wolf left its pack, and slowly and carefully approached a human being, touching the human's outstretched hand with its nose in a gesture of curiosity and trust. Similar bondings between wolves and humankind also occurred in other parts of the world around that same time.

No one really knows why this happened. Perhaps the human had some food to share. Or maybe humans had encroached on wolf territory, and the wolf was forced to interact out of self-preservation. Whatever the reason, this event forever changed the relationship between wolf and human being. Wolves gradually became, for some people, companions in which they put their love and trust. These wolves (which, when domesticated, became known as dogs) provided companionship, safety, and enjoyment for people. In return, people gave these wolves food and companionship. Both wolf and human have enjoyed a relationship since that time. Scientists now agree that all dogs, from Great Danes to the tiny Chihuahua, are all close relatives of the wolf (Johnson and Aamodt 1985).

Cats

Four thousand years ago in ancient Egypt, it was illegal to kill a cat. The punishment for doing so was death. Cats were worshipped by the Egyptians. Even Bastet, the Egyptian goddess of motherhood and fertility, took the shape of a cat. If you could go back through time and wander into an ordinary Egyptian home, you would see that every young Egyptian couple kept a statue of Bastet in their home, believing that this would ensure them many children.

Imagine this: Warring armies against Egypt were said to have used cats as shields, believing that the Egyptian soldiers would not harm the cats. Can you imagine fierce soldiers feeling more protected behind shields of fur rather than shields of armor? Who knows how true this is, but it is certainly a wonderful mythology and a testament to the reverence in which cats were held.

Some scholars believe that the original reason for the domestication of the cat stemmed from religious or spiritual beliefs, such as the worship of Bastet. Others say cats became household favorites for their excellent mouse- and rodent-catching abilities (Squire 2000).

Still others might say that the cat has never really been domesticated at all.

Birds

The history of the companionship between birds and humans has also been dated to approximately 4,000 years ago. It is unclear exactly which culture was the first to appreciate the special relationship a bird might have with a human, but we've been given some clues. Egyptian hieroglyphics frequently depict doves and parrots as pets. In India, the mynah bird has been considered sacred for about 2,000 years. Parakeets were kept as pets in Greek society, and in wealthy Roman homes, the parrot was the companion bird of choice. If you think about the high entertainment value of parrots, with their mimicking and often amusing snatches of sentences, you might realize that they were the early equivalent of watching television or listening to a radio.

As you can see, the human-animal bond has a long history. No matter what animal or animals you have chosen as your particular companion, one thing is certain, you are not alone. There are currently more than 63 million cats, 55 million dogs, 31 million birds, 3 million reptiles, and 12 million other small animals in people's homes, and these animals often play a crucial role in the lives of people around the world.

Activities: Where Did Your Pet Originate?

1. You may find it interesting and helpful to research the origin of your particular companion animal(s). If it's a dog, for example, even a mixed breed, how did the specific breed or breeds develop? If a bird, where did it originate? Where is it found in the wild today? What are some traits that are peculiar to the breed of your pet? (You might want to begin writing your journal entries or tape recording with this activity.)

Your local library or the Internet would be good places to start your search. Look for pictures that resemble your pet if you're unsure of the exact breed, then read the articles that accompany the photos. You might be surprised to learn that your companion animal has a rich history.

2. Why did you pick this particular companion animal to share your life with? What are the things you have especially liked and loved about your pet? Write a short paragraph or just make a list of the positive things you know your pet has brought into your life.

Attachment

If you have ever had the privilege of seeing a humpback whale breaching off the coast of Hawaii, or watching a bald eagle soaring high and proud over Alaskan forests, you may have an instinctive understanding of our human attachment to animals. As our lives have become more urbanized and isolated from nature, many of us want the experience of being a part of the lives of these other beings.

Obviously you're not going to cozy up to a whale or an eagle, but you may have a strong desire to be with animals that you can live with in harmony, or to catch even a glimpse of the wild, free-living being within us all. It's hard not to smile when you see a cat chasing a spider as if its life depended on it, or when you watch a dog that has developed the discipline to balance a treat on its nose, until given the command to eat it.

You might think that during our eons-long relationship with companion animals, we humans would have developed a special sensitivity to the loss of these "family" members. Yet, all too often, the news that our pet has died is met with comments like, "It's only a dog! Get over it. Go to the pound and get another one." Such responses demonstrate a socially sanctioned insensitivity to genuine human suffering. Comments such as these do not adequately respect the profound loss and the feelings of grief and bereavement that often accompany the death of a pet.

Before becoming a psychologist, I sold veterinary pharmaceuticals for Squibb Pharmaceutical Company's animal health division. Most of my time was spent in the waiting rooms of veterinary hospitals. Do you remember the last time you sat in the veterinarian's waiting room with your pet? Remember the sounds of the upset dogs and cats, the birds screeching, the staff scurrying around?

If you spoke to others in the waiting room, you probably heard their stories of why they were there. Or maybe you told a willing listener your story of your pet's woes. Such stories are important because they can help you to appreciate that you are not alone in the connection or attachment that you feel for your companion animal. Because there is still not a lot of societal support for the feelings you have for your beloved friend, you know you usually can find some comfort in talking with others who share the same feelings.

Twenty years ago, when I began working with people experiencing grief over the loss of a companion animal, veterinarians did not send the sympathy cards that are common today. Greeting-card companies didn't even make these types of cards. And although the level of sympathy is greater today than it was then, there still exists some uneasiness about admitting how much losing a pet can hurt.

If you have lost a companion animal, you may have felt or even still be feeling grief, loneliness, and perhaps some embarrassment about the depth of your pain. Many people feel that their pet is their best friend—perhaps their only friend. Your attachment is quite real, and whether people understand it or not, your grief is legitimate, and not as unusual as some might like you to believe it is.

What Is Attachment?

Let's define the word "attachment." In academic terms, attachment is a feeling of devotion that binds a person to another person, an animal, a thing, or a cause. For the purposes of this book, *attachment* means the experience of feeling bonded with or devoted to a companion animal. Remember, this attachment is neither new nor unique to just a few of us. It goes back thousands of years. It might even be that we, as human beings, are "hardwired" to form attachments to other humans, animals, or if need be, objects that we perceive as having humanlike qualities.

Did you see the movie *Castaway*, starring Tom Hanks? Hanks' character is stranded on a deserted island. There are no humans or animals, so he creates a somewhat humanlike character to talk to—and he creates it out of a volleyball. He names it Wilson (which is actually the name of the manufacturer stamped onto the volleyball), and he paints a face on it using his own blood. When the castaway tries to leave the island in his handmade raft, Wilson falls overboard, and Hanks cries for his loss. In fact, I noticed people in the theater crying when Wilson rolled away into the ocean.

An attachment to animals becomes problematic when the bond between guardian and pet becomes so strong that it excludes human attachments. In other words, when the pet becomes a person's whole world, human relationships may suffer or be relinquished altogether. Add to this the fact that companion animals usually don't live as long as humans; when they die, a huge void is created, especially when there is no one or nothing else to fill that void.

People often say that what they fear most is to be alone. In prisons, solitary confinement is considered the worst punishment that can be inflicted on a prisoner. Moreover, in some cultures and religions, those who commit heinous acts are isolated or "shunned." For members of these cultures, there is no greater form of punishment than being condemned to live as an outcast.

Attachment to someone or something seems to be a natural condition for humans and some domesticated animals. It is interesting to note that attachment and why it occurs, or doesn't, is the subject of countless theories and books. Scholars have written for years about what has been called "attachment theory." If you're curious about the depth of attachment theory, it might make an interesting subject for further study. There is no shortage of resources to examine, and a few of the better ones are listed in the Suggested Reading section at the back of this book.

A Shared Attachment

Let's consider another phenomenon that sometimes takes place between humans and animals. Many people (hundreds or even thousands) can become attached to the same animal. For example, on December 1, 2000, a twenty-nine-year-old orangutan named Ken Allen had to be euthanized at the San Diego Zoo. This primate had captured the imagination and won the attention of zoo-goers for many years. He was an accomplished escape artist and had managed to outwit the designers of his enclosure several times. Whenever Ken Allen escaped, he gleefully roamed the zoo grounds, much to the delight of his fans.

When Ken Allen became ill, no effort was spared to make him comfortable in his waning months, but finally he had to be euthanized.

The story of his death was front page news in *The San Diego Union-Tribune* (2000). A memorial service was held for him, and many people who had come every day to the zoo to see him were deeply distraught. Douglas G. Myers, executive director of the Zoological Society of San Diego, put it this way: "Ken Allen was a joy and a challenge. This is a difficult time for the keepers, a loss of family." Obviously, many people felt a deep attachment to this particular animal. It's also noteworthy that the zoo considered him to be a "family member."

There are times when your attachment to a companion animal may be perceived as even more important than any attachment you may feel for another human being. There can be many reasons for this perception. Some of these are as follows:

1. You may believe, or others might see, that your pet is or was your most significant source of emotional support.

2. You spend significant time and /or financial resources on long-term care for your pet.

3. Your companion animal is linked in your mind to significant people who have died or moved away, or perhaps to a marriage that has ended.

4. You live in a small family group or with no children. Thus, you are seen as more attached to your pets than those who live in larger households.

Perhaps the most important thing to remember about attachment is that it is a normal and very human response. It may also help to remember that you are in the company of people who acknowledged and appreciated the bond between animals and humans thousands of years ago.

Activity: How Do or Did You Feel About Your Pet?

There are many levels of attachment or bonding that will be discussed in depth in the next chapter. However, you might want to take this opportunity to think about your own attachment to your companion animal(s). Why have they been so special to you? Are your pets part of your family? Do you feel more attached to them than you do to any people?

Make a list of the ways in which you think you give your companion animal extra attention, ways such as preparing special foods, sharing your thoughts verbally, or lavishing attention—anything you don't normally do for other people in your life.

The Benefits of Bonding

Although the bond between humans and domesticated animals goes back thousands of years, research into the benefits of this relationship is relatively new. One of the first studies on the physiological benefits of pet guardianship was carried out at the University of Maryland from 1977 to 1979 (Friedman, Katcher, Lynch, and Thomas 1980). The purpose of the study was to look at the one-year survival rates of people who had had heart attacks. The study included every variable known to be associated with mortality from heart disease. Almost as an afterthought, pet guardianship was also included as a variable, although many of the researchers in this study joked about it. However, when all of the data had been accumulated, a surprising result was demonstrated.

It seemed that the only statistically significant difference between those who survived for longer than a year and those who didn't was pet guardianship. Of course, as you might imagine, the researchers were more than a little skeptical. They reasoned that perhaps the beneficial factor was exercise, and because dog guardians usually walk their dogs, the researchers thought that what they were really looking at was exercise. So, they reran the data, only this time they omitted those who had dogs. Guess what? The results were the same. Pet guardianship did indeed have a direct correlation with one-year survival rates after heart surgery.

After this initial study was completed, more evidence began to emerge that pets are good for your health. For example, many studies demonstrated that petting your animal can lower your blood pressure. It's also interesting to note that your companion animal's blood pressure also falls when it is being petted, thus making the relationship healthy for both (Beck and Katcher 1996).

If you think health benefits are confined to petting cats and dogs, think again. Watching fish can relieve anxiety; it can be a deeply meditative process, and, for some people, is almost hypnotic. In one of the more expensive hotels in Las Vegas, you will find a giant aquarium behind the check-in counter. Although beautiful, its purpose is not entirely esthetic; it is also there to keep you distracted and calm while you are standing in long lines waiting to check in. Obviously, the hotel executives did some research on the physiological and psychological benefits of aquariums. Since this information has become more widely known, I've begun to see aquariums popping up in restaurants, doctors' waiting rooms, and office buildings.

An Australian study found that people with companion animals had lower serum cholesterol and triglyceride levels than those who had no pets in their lives (Anderson, Warwick, Reid, and Jennings 1992). The study found no differences in the health habits of the two sets of people. To me, this is pretty amazing. Although pets should never be a substitute for proper nutrition, healthy exercise, and regular physical check-ups, it would seem that they add to our lives in a very significant way—they keep us healthier.

So far, I have mentioned only the physiological benefits of pet guardianship. What about the psychological benefits? They, too, are numerous. Animals act as great "humor therapists," often providing us with the laughter we might not find in our everyday lives. Animals lack the inhibitions that most humans have, and they can be endlessly amusing just by being themselves. And as *Readers' Digest* has suggested time and again, laughter is the best medicine. It is a natural stress-buster, causing the brain to release the endorphins that give us a sense of well-being.

Companion animals offer love and companionship, relationships that many of us do not receive from human beings. Pets provide us with a feeling of security. Don't you feel safer if you have a dog or perhaps a snake in your home? Animals also have a way of bringing out the best in many of us. You've probably noticed that people are friendlier and more apt to speak to you while you are walking your dog, thus giving you a common ground to meet new friends. Where I live, in California, we have dog parks and beaches. People bring their pets to interact with each other and their human guardians.

It seems nowadays that every large city has dog parks and/or dog runs. They are places where everyone has fun and no one feels inferior or superior because of social or economic status. For many of us, our pets are like our children. Small wonder we feel a profound loss when we lose them.

Activity: List the Advantages of Having a Pet

I have mentioned only a few of the many physiological and psychological advantages of companion animals. Perhaps you might like to add to my comments by writing a list of your own, so that you can see how much your particular pet really does for you. Once you do this, you will understand more deeply why you become so sad when you lose these teachers and healers.

Popular Culture and Attachment

According to an article in *Psychology Today* (Lachman 2000) nearly 70 percent of the 80 million pet guardians in the United States say they give their critters as much attention as they do their children. Therefore, it shouldn't surprise us that animals are widely used to sell products, keep us entertained, and gain insight into our own selves.

The creative people in the entertainment industry, as well as those in advertising, are very much aware of the attachment between humans and their pets. Animals are prominently featured in television, films, advertisements, and greeting cards so that people will associate the animal with the movie, program, or product. Savvy marketing executives use the principles of attachment theory to help their industry gain viewers, listeners, or product users of all ages.

Many of you will remember the television show *Lassie*, in which the beautiful collie Lassie was always there to help his family out of trouble. And Disneyland employs Mickey Mouse as its "main man." The movies are filled with animals, both as stars and as peripheral members of the cast. Who can forget *Lady and the Tramp*, the animated movie featuring two dogs falling in love over a plate of spaghetti? Or how about *The Incredible Journey*, the story of two dogs and a cat who together traveled thousands of miles to reunite with their beloved guardian? Let's not forget the music industry. The Beatles' songs "Blackbird" and "Rocky Raccoon" certainly make these characters seem alive and human-like. Or have you ever heard the old song "Mr. Bojangles," by Jerry Jeff Walker? The lyrics describe Mr. Bojangles' dog, who one day just "up and died," and after twenty years Mr. Bojangles still grieves for his lost friend.

Books also depict animals in all sorts of ways, often giving them human characteristics. Remember the Cheshire Cat in *Alice in Wonderland*, or the sensitive, brave rabbits in *Watership Down*? Orwell's classic *Animal Farm* used animals to describe the inequities of humans' interactions in political and social systems. Hundreds of books tell fictional or historical tales of an animal's life. Perhaps you can recall the ones that touched you when you were a child, or even as an adult (think *Bambi* or *Free Willy*). Certainly, cartoons have entertained us for a long time, with animal characters like Wiley Coyote often giving us fresh insights into human behavior.

Politicians and celebrities know the value of companion animals, not only for the experience of having a trustworthy companion, but also for their popularity with the public, or even the lack thereof, as former President Lyndon B. Johnson found out, to his dismay. On May 8, 1964, President Johnson was shown on the cover of *Time* magazine picking up his pet beagle by its ears. The White House was flooded with thousands of angry telegrams and phone calls from the public. Johnson may have received more complaints about that photograph than he did for his role in America's participation in the Vietnam War.

Most presidents either already have a dog when they are elected or they acquire one while holding the office. Richard Nixon had Checkers; George Bush, Sr., had Millie, who made the cover of *Life* magazine when she had puppies. Bill Clinton started out with a cat, Socks, but the public wasn't too interested in Socks because, true to his cat nature, Socks was not about to perform for us. So what did Clinton do? He got himself a chocolate Labrador, Buddy, a much better political animal. And George W. Bush. has two dogs, Barney and Spotty, thus outdoing all previous presidents, as far as having "gone to the dogs."

Celebrities are not immune from the appeal of our animal friends. Betty White and Carol Burnett have been very outspoken about their love of companion animals. At a convention I attended some years ago, Ms. White was on stage with the golden retriever that played Shadow in the Disney movie *The Incredible Journey*. While she was eloquently speaking about the many virtues of companion animals, the dog barked. She quipped back to him, "You have no speaking lines in this speech." Shadow proceeded to look hurt and quieted down. At another event, singer-songwriter James Taylor brought his small dog on stage with him, and the dog helped Mr. Taylor sing a song. I have to admit, though, that I preferred Taylor's voice by itself, but still, it was a triumph for the human-animal bond!

Clearly, advertising companies know that animals sell products. Glance at any magazine or watch an hour of network television and you might be surprised by how many commercials feature animals. As I write this, I just received a Land's End clothing catalog. On the front cover there are six photos of people placed next to six photos of dogs. The title is "Great Go-togethers." What's striking about the photos is that the humans' physical features look amazingly similar to their dogs' features, and vice versa. This is great creative advertising. And, of course, Smoky the Bear and Woodsy Owl have long been used as symbols to protect the environment, helping us to remember important lessons that we might forget without them.

Now that you have read a little about the history of the human-animal connection, are you surprised by how thoroughly images of animals have saturated our lives and culture? It's no wonder we are so attached to our companion animals. Such bonding is normal, given the long history of the human-animal bond and the prevalence of animals in our lives. I believe that, when you understand the history of our attachment to animals, you will better understand the roots of your own attachment.

As you move on to the next chapter, you will be given tools to recognize and assess your own attachment to your companion animal. Once you understand the depth of your bond, it will become easier for you to understand why it hurts so much when your companion is no longer in your life.

Activities: Important Animals in Your Life

1. In your journal, or on your tape recorder, you might want to make a list of the books, television shows, songs, and movies with animals as their theme that have touched your life. What about these stories touched you? Why did you enjoy, or not enjoy them?

2. If you have children or nieces and nephews, look for books that will help them understand the enjoyment of an animal friend.

3. Make a scrapbook, photo album, or video of your companion animal. You might want to write a short story to go with this, much as a screenwriter would do. What will your story say? What photos or videos will you use? What would be your message?

Chapter 2

Bonding: From the Conventional to the Unique

*When we look into each other's eyes, she is very human.
It is like having a child, but a child with a terrific sense
of humor.*

—Jack Lemmon, describing Chloe,
his black standard poodle

Think back to when you were a child. You probably had many toys, but maybe you remember a special one, the toy that was your favorite. Perhaps it was an old doll, or a teddy bear that you dragged with you wherever you went. It was your faithful companion, and you hugged it close whenever you felt sad or alone. Remember Linus, from the comic strip *Peanuts*? He clung to his beloved blanket tenaciously and he panicked whenever he was separated from it, even briefly. His blanket gave him the comfort he needed to deal with the daily challenges of childhood.

That feeling of attachment to a cherished toy or an object that you had as a child can be experienced as an adult, too, as the feeling of attachment you have for your companion animals. The *degree* of attachment that is felt, however, varies widely among people, and it is that degree that will affect the depth of the grief you experience when you lose your pet.

Types of Bonding

When people tell me about losing a companion animal, if I can determine the strength of their emotional attachment, it becomes much easier for me to understand the depth of their grief and how long it might last. During my fifteen years of helping people cope with losing a pet, I have noticed that animal lovers fall into one of three general categories. For the purpose of my discussion I have labeled these categories as:

1. Conventionally bonded

2. Intensely bonded

3. Uniquely bonded

In this chapter you will learn to identify the characteristics of each type of bonding. Then you will be asked to complete a short worksheet to help you determine the type of bond you share with your pet. Understanding the depth of your bond will help you to move through your grieving process more easily.

Conventionally Bonded

Conventionally bonded animal lovers consider their pets as members of their families, but they don't give their pets the same status they do to their human family members. These folks make up the largest group of pet guardians. They provide loving homes and are responsible about caring for their pets, but losing a pet is not a source of major trauma. Although they experience grief over the loss of a pet, people in this category tend to recover more quickly than intensely or uniquely bonded people.

Intensely Bonded

Pet guardians who are intensely bonded regard their pets as integral family members. They form deep, emotional attachments to their pets and provide them with the same level of care they would for any other family member. Intensely bonded pet guardians may sometimes exceed their financial means to provide care for their pets. They even may think of their companion animal as their "surrogate child." Intensely bonded pet owners often experience a long grieving process and a much greater sense of personal loss following the loss of their pet than conventionally bonded pet owners.

Uniquely Bonded

People with the deepest attachment to their companion animals, those who are uniquely bonded, provide extravagant care and attention to their pets. Often, they prefer the company of their pets to that of other humans, and they may even refer to their pet by such terms as "my closest friend," "my soul mate," "my son," or "my daughter." The loss of their close companion often is devastating, and their grieving may last for a very long time.

You may already be developing a general idea of which category best describes you, but how will knowing the level of your bonding help you to understand your grief? The answer is, that when you can identify the level of your bonding, you will know what to expect during the entire grieving process. Often, when people are grieving, they think that their reactions are atypical, or somehow abnormal, or that they are losing their minds. It's comforting and validating to learn that many others experience the same feelings you're having.

Also, knowing that people bond with different levels of intensity can help you to understand and accept others' reactions. Say, for example, you are grieving deeply for a pet, but you feel abandoned by your family and friends who don't sympathize with your intense emotions. Understanding that their reactions, though different from yours, are just as valid as yours can guide you to seek the support that you need.

Or, imagine that you are a family member who is surprised at the extreme pain and loss felt by another person in your family, and you're finding it difficult to help that person. In both cases, the information in this chapter will help you to clarify your feelings and will reveal how you can best deal with those feelings.

Pet Attachment Worksheet (PAW)

Your first step is to determine the actual level of bonding you experience with your pet. Answer the questions on the following worksheet and calculate your score. Then we will explore each level of bonding more deeply.

Pet Attachment Worksheet (PAW)

Please answer each of the following questions as honestly as you can, in terms of how you feel *right now*. There aren't any right or wrong answers. All that matters is that you express your true thoughts on each question. In this worksheet, "companion animals" and "pets" mean the same thing. If you have more than one pet, you might wish to repeat the PAW for each one, replacing the general term "pet" or "pets" with each pet's name.

Please respond to the questions by writing the number of your answer in the space provided. Use the following scale to record your answers on the right-hand side of each question.

1	2	3	4	5	6	7
Strongly Disagree	Moderately Disagree	Slightly Disagree	Unsure	Slightly Agree	Moderately Agree	Strongly Agree

1. I really like seeing pets enjoy their food. ____

2. My pet means more to me than any of my friends. ____

3. I would like a pet in my home. ____

4. Having pets is not a waste of money. ____

5. Companion animals add happiness to my life. ____

6. I spend time every day playing with my pet(s). ____

7. I have occasionally communicated with my pet and understood what it was trying to express. ____

8. The world would be a better place if people spent as much time caring for their companion animals as they do for other humans. ＿＿＿

9. I like to feed animals out of my hand. ＿＿＿

10. I love pets. ＿＿＿

11. Pets are fun and are worth the expense and trouble that they may create. ＿＿＿

12. I frequently talk to my pet. ＿＿＿

13. I love animals. ＿＿＿

14. You should treat your pets with as much respect as you would a human member of your family. ＿＿＿

15. My pet is my best friend. ＿＿＿

16. I like my pet to sleep with me (or would like it if my pet was small enough). ＿＿＿

17. It's okay for my pet to eat at the table with me. ＿＿＿

18. My pet understands me better than any human in my life does. ＿＿＿

19. I expect unconditional love from my pet. ＿＿＿

20. Animals belong in the home as much as they do in the wild. ＿＿＿

Adapted, with permission, from The Pet Attitude Scale by Donald I. Templer, Ph.D., California School of Professional Psychology, Fresno

Now that you have completed the worksheet, add up the numbers that you wrote down on the right-hand side for each question. For example, if you wrote number 6 for the first question and number 7 for the second, you would have a score of 13 for the first two questions. If you answered Strongly Agree for all twenty questions you would have a total score of 140. Remember that PAW scores fall along a continuum, so the following labels are not as important as your own personal bond. Nevertheless, your score should give you a good idea of your attachment to your pet.

My PAW score is: ＿＿＿＿＿＿＿＿＿

Those who have no particular attachment to pets will score below 35. Conventionally bonded pet owners will find their scores somewhere between 35 and 98. A score between 98 and 125 places you in the intensely bonded range, and a score between 125 and 140 is probably an indication of a unique bond between you and your companion animal. With either of the latter two levels of bonding, you will probably experience a long and intense time of grieving.

Whatever your level of bonding may be, later chapters will give you tools and activities to meet your specific needs and help to ease you through your grieving.

Conventionally Bonded Pet Guardians

If you are conventionally bonded, you give loving and responsible care to your pets. You provide good food, a place to sleep, and some amount of attention. Your pets see the veterinarian for regular exams and for treatment of any medical conditions that might occur. You may consider your pets as part of your extended family, although only as peripheral members, and they don't enjoy the same status as your human family members.

After losing a pet, you would normally experience a shorter and less intense grieving process than other, more deeply bonded owners. You appreciate your companion animals but do not generally form deep emotional attachments or dependent bonds with them. Thus, you tend to recover more easily from their loss. After holding a memorial service for your animal, you might get another pet in a few weeks. The following story illustrates a couple who were conventionally bonded with their dog.

Bill and Judy

Bill, a thirty-eight-year-old dentist, lives with his wife, Judy, and their two kids in a big house in the suburbs outside of Kansas City. Their friendly golden retriever, Busby, spent most of his time in the backyard, curled up on the patio or barking at the kids going back and forth from school. Busby especially liked Saturdays, when the family cooked hamburgers on the grill, Judy gardened, and the kids played games. Lots of activity took place in the backyard on weekends, and Busby boisterously enjoyed all of it.

Busby participated in family activities *only* when it was convenient and pleasurable for the family. What differentiates these conventionally bonded guardians from those with deeper attachments is that they do not look at things from the animal's perspective. As you can see from this story, Busby enjoyed the time that the family spent with him, the Saturday barbecue, the kids playing, and Judy's gardening. These activities brought pleasure to the family, and Busby was allowed to participate in them, but he also spent long periods of time alone.

When Busby was a puppy and was left alone in the backyard, he had wanted to join the family indoors, and he sometimes scratched on the door and barked to be let in. But he quickly learned that was not to be. He had a comfortable doghouse of his own, and he was normally left outside to entertain himself. Bill, Judy, and their children did not often react to their dog's requests for attention, unless the dog's wishes fit in with their schedules or when they involved basic necessities, such as food or medical attention.

Conventionally bonded pet owners do not often take into account their pet's desires, and this often indicates a certain absence of emotional connection on the humans' side. Busby's connection to the family was much stronger than the humans' connection to Busby. One important element of a conventionally bonded relationship is that the pet guardian gains much more from it than the animal does. However, conventionally bonded owners believe that their pets are getting as much attention as they need. On the PAW scale they are somewhere between nonbonded people, who tend to believe that animals have no emotional needs at all, and intensely bonded people, who believe that animals are quite like people in that they have emotional lives and emotional needs.

When Busby began to have trouble breathing, Bill and Judy took him to the veterinarian where they discovered that Busby's heart was failing. His difficulty breathing came from fluid building up in his lungs. Daily medication eased his problems for a year or so, but, eventually, Busby's breathing became uncomfortably ragged.

"He tried to play with the kids," Judy said, "but he could barely breathe. I gave him his pill every day, but after a while it didn't do any good. One Saturday afternoon, we took him to the vet to be put out of his misery. I cried. I really do miss him."

Judy's grief was genuine, even though the level of her emotional bond to Busby was not as strong as those of intensely bonded people to their pets. But Busby had been a part of her life, and his loss left a void. Her grieving was not likely be lengthy, but the sorrow she felt when she described his death was profound.

I suggested the following steps for her to take to deal with the immediate feelings of grief she was experiencing:

1. Judy and her family held a simple memorial service for Busby in their backyard, where they had shared many happy times together.

2. Judy put Busby's doghouse, toys, blanket, and food dish away in the garage. She did this because every time she caught sight of something of Busby's, it caused her to feel a fresh pang of

sadness. With these reminders out of sight, she wouldn't have the constant stabs of sadness.

3. Judy had had a routine every morning, in which she got out of bed, fed Busby, made coffee, and took a shower. So, when she would normally be feeding Busby, instead of rekindling her feelings of grief she changed her routine and slipped into some comfortable clothing as soon as she awoke, and went for a short walk.

Within a week or two, Judy's feelings of loss began to diminish, and remembrances of Busby were producing fond smiles rather than grief.

Intensely Bonded Pet Guardians

If you determined that you fall within the range of the intensely bonded, you probably go to great efforts to provide loving care for your pets. It wouldn't be unusual for you to consider your companion animals as full family members. I often hear from intensely bonded people that they spend time researching commercial pet foods or even preparing their pet's food from basic raw ingredients rather than buying commercially prepared foods. If you have cats, you might buy or build special cat furniture, taking extra efforts to enrich your cats' lives.

You typically "go the extra mile" to provide the best veterinary care available for your pet, and you might be willing to spend more than you can afford for special medical procedures or treatments. The result of your doing all of these things is the formation of deep, emotional attachments with your companion animals. Because you care more deeply for your pets than those who have lower scores on the PAW scale, you tend to experience an extended period of time grieving and a much greater sense of personal loss following the death of your pet. You shouldn't find this surprising, because your pet shared very close emotional ties with you and played a major part in your life.

Let's look at an example of a couple who experienced intense bonding with their cat.

Janie and Greg

When Janie and Greg Richards, a couple in their late twenties, found they were unable to have children, they came to regard their cat as their surrogate child. Sadie slept with them and spent the evening curled up on Janie's lap while Janie watched television. Raised on high-quality food from a pet store and kept indoors, Sadie enjoyed a long and healthy life, until at the age of seventeen, she began urinating outside of her litter box. When Janie noticed the reddish tinge to Sadie's urine, Greg and Janie together took Sadie to the veterinarian. There, they found that their beloved pet had developed chronic kidney disease.

Greg readily agreed to give Sadie her daily treatment of subcutaneous fluids, which required him to insert a small needle into the loose skin on her back and drip fluids from an IV bag into her body, to increase her fluids and rehydrate her body. Sadie lived two more years, gradually becoming thinner and weaker, but she still retained her sunny spirit.

"Even during the last few months, she loved to be petted and to lie in the sun," Janie remembered. "When I held her in the evening, she purred for me, even on the day when we had to take her to the veterinarian for the last time. I don't know how we will be able to get through Christmas. She came to live with us at Christmas time. She used to play with the ornaments on the tree and broke almost every one, but we didn't care! We loved to watch her play. She brought such joy into our lives. We buried her in our backyard and planted a special rose bush over her grave."

Childless couples often fit into the intensely bonded category because their companion animal may fill the role of a child. But regardless of your situation, married or single, providing a safe and loving environment for a small, dependent creature satisfies a deep human need, and offers an outlet for your nurturing, parental skills. At the same time, the companion animal returns your care and affection with the unconditional love and acceptance of a young child. Sadie's happy disposition lit up Greg and Janie's everyday world with joy and playfulness.

Janie and Greg not only lost a companion animal that was like a child to them, they also nursed Sadie through a long, debilitating illness. If you have experienced this, you know it takes a tremendous physical and emotional toll. (See chapter 5 for a discussion about caring for a chronically ill companion animal.)

Once your pet is gone, the arrival of holidays or special events that you shared may make you feel even sadder. A change of routine for the holidays might be the best thing you can do after you lose a pet. Consider visiting family members in a distant location or doing something else that won't magnify the absence of your companion animal. You also might want to avoid going to the park where you often walked with your dog.

Janie expressed dread at the approach of Christmas because that was when Sadie had first come to live with them, and her memory of that joyful time was especially strong. Janie and Greg instinctively performed one important act for coping with their pain. They planted a rose bush over Sadie's grave. In chapter 3 you'll find many other suggestions such as creating a scrapbook, poem, or song to remember your pet by, or donating to a good cause in your pet's name.

Uniquely Bonded Pet Guardians

If you found yourself at the upper end of the PAW scale, you probably provide lavish care and attention to your pets. It wouldn't be unusual for you to regard them as having equal status with members of your human family. For most people who are uniquely bonded with their pets, something in their background led to their becoming so attached to their companion animals. Other people may have hurt them, either in childhood or as adults, so they feel safer and more comfortable establishing deep emotional bonds with their animal companions.

If you are uniquely bonded, you may think of your pet as your child, referring to him or her as your "son" or "daughter," or even as your "significant other." Developing trusting relationships with other people may be extremely difficult for you. Often, such trust issues have their roots in early childhood losses or trauma.

Unique attachments also form for those of you who depend on a working dog, such as a Seeing Eye canine for help walking or navigating. Obviously, these animals provide more than the usual benefits of pet guardianship because they act as an extension of your physical body, resulting in an even more intimate and dependent relationship.

If you are uniquely bonded, you have developed extremely close attachments to your companion animals and you react acutely to your pet's death, experiencing a profound process of grieving. This makes sense; in fact, the unique nature of your attachment almost demands it. However, as with almost all prolonged grief over the loss of a pet, society frequently does not regard your pain as "legitimate" grief. This may make your time of grieving even more difficult.

Now, let's take a look at a case study to illustrate unique bonding.

Charlotte and Bonsai

Some time ago, I received a call from a woman who told me, with obvious emotion in her voice, that she had just lost her son. I suggested that she might want to come in and talk about it.

An attractive woman in her forties, Charlotte had tears in her eyes when she walked into my office. We hadn't gotten too far into the session when I realized that the son she was mourning was her Akita dog, Bonsai.

Charlotte spent most of the first session crying, speaking with great difficulty. When she could speak, this is what she said:

"Bonsai went everywhere with me. The veterinarians did all they could, but I still feel that we could have done more." Although Bonsai had been gone for five months, Charlotte's pain would not subside. Her husband, Todd, had also loved Bonsai, but his grief had begun to lessen. He was frustrated and increasingly perplexed at his wife's continuing sorrow. He wanted his happy wife back again. Over the next three months we met weekly, and Charlotte's history came out slowly and painfully as we developed a trusting relationship.

Bonsai had been diagnosed with cancer at the age of ten. Charlotte and Todd had obtained the best veterinary care available, including surgery and chemotherapy, but the dog didn't make it.

"Bonsai's heart just gave out," Charlotte said.

When I asked Charlotte to talk to me a little bit about her past she told me that she had met Todd during her senior year of college. After graduation, they married and they soon adopted Bonsai, then an eight-month-old Akita puppy.

Because Todd worked late many nights, Bonsai was her sole companion during the day and many evenings. Early in their marriage, Charlotte and Todd had decided not to have children, so Bonsai became their "son." They loved him greatly and took him everywhere, even on their vacations.

Charlotte also told me about another dog, Frisky, who had meant a great deal to her in her childhood. As she talked about her early life, I began to see why she was so uniquely bonded to Bonsai. Her parents had separated when she was quite young, and during the ensuing bitter custody battle, her father had spirited her away from her mother and moved to a distant part of the country. Each time detectives hired by her mother found them, Charlotte and her dad moved again.

Her father had no difficulty finding work wherever they moved, but his jobs often required him to work long hours, which forced Charlotte to turn to Frisky for the unconditional love and security that she craved and needed. Unable to form lasting friendships with other children because of the nearly constant moving, Charlotte became shy, and eventually she stopped trying to make friends at all.

Charlotte remembered, as a nine-year-old, having Frisky kiss her favorite doll every morning before she left for school. Then she took the doll to school with her because its presence helped her to feel more secure. Every day she went straight home from school to play with Frisky until her dad came home.

At the age of eighteen, Charlotte left her father and moved away to college, leaving Frisky with him. Two weeks after she left, Frisky died.

Because she was so preoccupied with all of the other changes in her life, she didn't have time to think very much about Frisky's death, even though the dog had meant so much to her.

For many people, losing a companion animal can open the psyche to traumatic losses suffered in the past. That was surely the case with Charlotte's profound grief. Her deep sorrow was triggered by Bonsai's death, but it also brought to the surface many of the buried memories from her past: Frisky's death, not mourned at the time, her lonely childhood, and the early forced separation from her mother.

Clearly, the length and intensity of her bereavement placed her at the upper end of the PAW scale.

As an adult, Charlotte's reliance on Bonsai had parallels with her childhood relationship with Frisky. Left alone most of the time as a child and later as a wife, she learned to rely on dogs for companionship and security. She gave as much love to Frisky and Bonsai as she received from them. This elevated them to higher than mere animal status, which is why uniquely bonded people tend to think of companion animals as human beings.

How can you tell if you are uniquely bonded to your companion animals rather than intensely bonded? Since the intensity of human attachment to companion animals is one of degree, I don't like to draw a rigid distinction between the two groups. However, the key characteristic that best distinguishes the uniquely bonded from the intensely bonded is the degree to which they *anthropomorphize*—that is, the degree to which they assign human characteristics to animals.

Whether we admit it or not, most of us who have pets talk to them on occasion, and sometimes we attribute complex human thinking and emotions to them. But people who are intensely bonded do not believe that their companion animals really have the human characteristics they ascribe to them. They know that they are exaggerating. Also, they don't see their relationship with a companion animal as equal in value to that of their relationships with other humans.

On the other hand, people who are uniquely bonded with their companion animals strongly anthropomorphize them—they really do believe that their pets exhibit humanlike emotions and thoughts. They regard their relationship with their pets as equivalent to close relationships with human beings. Remember, Charlotte described Bonsai's death as losing her son.

Charlotte's husband, who was more intensely bonded than uniquely bonded with their dog, had some difficulty accepting the amount and degree of pain that Charlotte showed over Bonsai's loss. Todd had moved through the stages of the grief process, and he was perplexed about Charlotte's seeming inability to move through her own grief. Charlotte and Todd together had buried Bonsai and held a funeral service. They had put flowers on his grave, written a poem, and put together a scrapbook with a picture of Bonsai on the cover. Todd's grief over Bonsai eventually subsided. But Charlotte's did not.

This is one of the major differences between intensely and uniquely bonded individuals. The uniquely bonded person's grieving process lasts longer, usually because it is complicated by other factors.

So, Charlotte needed some additional tools to deal with her grief. This is what we developed to help her. At some point in every day, Charlotte conducted a ritual of remembering Bonsai and the happy moments they had shared. She sat at his grave for a few moments, thinking about him and remembering his happy life. And she kept going to therapy, whereas her husband did not.

The other issues that had made her so uniquely attached to Bonsai, that is, the loss of her mother and her childhood loneliness, were brought to the forefront, and Charlotte began to deal with them. She tried to take pleasure in simple things, things that she hadn't been able to enjoy during the time of Bonsai's illness and the months following his death. As time passed, she began to feel pleasure again. She found that even the smallest act, like having a cup of coffee while sitting out in the sun, could bring her pleasure.

Finally, Charlotte adopted a new Akita puppy, whom she named Bib. She and Todd chose the name Bib as an acronym for "Bonsai Is Beautiful" as a way to honor and memorialize their beloved Bonsai. As time goes by, Charlotte has become more attached to Bib. However, she continues to truly believe that one day she will see Bonsai again.

Activity: Your Thoughts and Feelings

Does anything about Charlotte's story touch you by reminding you of situations in your own life? If so, write about it, or talk to someone about your thoughts and feelings. Make it a pleasurable experience by taking your notebook, journal, or tape recorder to a comfortable corner indoors or to a beautifully scenic spot outside. Bring along a cup of tea or a soft drink, settle in, and write or speak from your heart. You might be surprised at what flows from your inner self.

If you cannot do this activity now, don't worry. You can come back to it later.

Nonbonded Pet Guardians

If you scored at the lower end of the PAW scale, you may be reading this book to understand someone else's grief. You may live with animals, but you probably do not have strong emotions when they die or must be given up. You may believe that animals don't have emotions, certainly not the kind of emotions that people have. When faced with someone grieving over the loss of a pet, you might be tempted to say, "You are being silly. It's only an animal!"

If that is the case, and if you are reading this book for someone else, you are to be commended for caring enough to learn about the emotional bonds between humans and companion animals. You may want to refer directly to chapter 10 for ideas that may help you in reaching out to a loved one who is suffering because she or he has lost a beloved pet.

Different Bonds Among Several Pets

If you have more than one companion animal, you may feel more emotionally connected to one than to another. Some people feel guilty about this, thinking that they should feel exactly the same feelings for each pet. However, many people experience a "special" connection with one particular animal. This doesn't mean that you don't love the others; there are many reasons you may feel especially connected to a certain pet.

For example, I rescued a three-week-old kitten from a Dumpster sixteen years ago. She was a scrawny thing, flea-ridden and mite-infested. I got up every few hours throughout the night to bottle-feed her, and she cried all night, unless I remained at her side. I named her Tara. This tiny creature followed me everywhere, the way a dog might, but she ran from anyone else. She still does. She always looks at me with adoration as if to say, "Thank you for rescuing me." Although I have another cat, Bosco, whom also I love dearly, Tara is my favorite. She has been my close companion for sixteen years.

Our close bond has grown out of a two-way relationship in which she gains as much from the relationship as I do. Ever since I pulled her from the Dumpster, Tara has looked upon me with special trust and affection. When she was a tiny kitten, she probably saw me as a maternal figure. Undoubtedly, I feel a corresponding maternal love based on our shared experiences of the nighttime feedings and her initial miserable condition.

I know that when I lose Tara, my grief will be deeper and longer lasting than it will be for Bosco. I have a great deal of love for Bosco and I do my best for her, but I'm not as attached to her as I am to Tara. Maybe it's because I didn't "rescue" Bosco in the same way that I rescued Tara, and I don't have that same maternal connection. In some ways, Tara is like a special-needs child for whom I feel extremely protective.

Why is this difference in bonding among multiple companion animals important? It's important for two reasons. First, you should understand that when you lose a pet you are closely attached to, your grieving process is likely to last longer and to be more profound. Acknowledging the differences in your level of bonding will help you to understand the differences in the severity of your grief.

Second, the differences in the strength of the bonding can produce guilty thoughts in pet guardians that can surface even before a pet is lost. You may be surprised to learn that most people, especially those who are intensely and uniquely bonded, experience a wide range of guilt about their relationships with their companion animals. Often, no matter how much guardians provide for their pets, they think they could do more. Because guilt in itself is such a strong emotion and has such a significant role in the grieving process, it is discussed in detail in chapter 4. But, for now, it is important to understand that guilty thoughts are common, particularly when you have a stronger bond with one pet over another.

Different Bonds in the Same Family

If one person in your family is uniquely bonded to a particular animal, and another person is intensely or conventionally bonded, their symptoms, and their grief, may be quite different. The more uniquely bonded, the more intense the grief will be.

Remember Charlotte and Todd's story? They had a distinct difference in the level of their bonding to Bonsai, and Todd had to struggle to understand why Charlotte's time of grieving was so extended. If you were uniquely bonded with your lost pet, as Charlotte was, you may not receive the respect or support that you would like or expect from those close to you. If that were to happen and you were to feel so misunderstood and isolated from your loved ones, it might tear you apart.

Here are some suggestions that might bring you closer:

Do some activities together, even if you don't feel like doing them. For example, if you are uniquely bonded, choose a particular time of the day to grieve, as Charlotte did. Then, at the end of that time, put the thoughts of your beloved companion animal aside. Do something with other family members that you all enjoy, such as going to a movie (Advice Note: Select a happy movie.) Treat the family to dinner at your favorite restaurant, go ice skating, or spend an afternoon at the beach.

I do not recommend going to the zoo or walking in the park where you often took your dog. Select something to do with your family that you all enjoy doing, which does not bring back memories of the lost pet. This will allow you and your loved ones to stay connected while you (or the person who is uniquely bonded) continues going through a long and difficult grieving process.

If you find it difficult to get the support you need from your partner or other family members, you may want to look for a pet-loss support group, which, typically, will have more uniquely bonded members than intensely or conventionally bonded people in it. The Internet is a treasure trove of sites for pet-loss support. Log on to a Web site chat room, and talk with folks who have the empathy that you are seeking.

If you are the one who is finding it difficult to understand the more intense emotions of another family member or a friend, remember the wide range of bonding represented by the PAW scale. Allow yourself to accept the legitimacy of the other person's grief. Remember, in extreme cases, the person experiencing what seems to be an unusually long time of grieving may feel as if a child has been lost. Certainly none of us would expect someone who has lost a human child to bounce "back to normal" in a few months. Encourage your friend or family member to follow the suggestions for coping with grief, and provide as much emotional and practical support as you are able.

By now, you should have a clear understanding of where you fall on the PAW scale and how the level of attachment you had for your pet directly affects your grieving process. Identifying your bonding level will help you immensely in applying the information to come to your own situation.

If you are a less-bonded person seeking insight into a loved one's deeper grief, understanding the very real differences in the levels of bonding will help you begin to peel away the layers of confusion surrounding grief. By now, a deep and prolonged grief should be less of a mystery to you, and you are well equipped to move forward in helping your loved one.

Chapter 3

Saying Good-bye

We who choose to surround ourselves with lives even more temporary than our own live within a fragile circle, easily and often breached. Unable to accept its awful gaps, we still would have it no other way. We cherish memory as the only certain immortality, never fully understanding the necessary plan. . . .

—Irving Townsend, from *The Once Again Prince*

"I'm sorry, we did everything we could for Teke, but we couldn't save him," Dr. Valentine told Howard.

"What do you mean, you couldn't save him?" Howard responded angrily. "Are you sure you have the right chart? I'm a doctor, you know, and mix-ups do happen. Perhaps you'd better check again."

Dr. Valentine sighed quietly, knowing that he had the right chart, but also knowing that Howard's reaction was typical. Howard was experiencing the beginning feelings of the grieving process

"Perhaps you'd like to go into the back of the hospital with me, and see if maybe I *have* made a mistake," Dr. Valentine said.

Howard agreed, although the first inklings of reality were beginning to sink in. It was probably true, Howard realized; Teke was gone. How ironic, he thought, I've said the same thing, hundreds of times, to many people, and they always had the same reaction I'm having. Now I know how they must have felt.

As they walked the length of the hospital, Howard reflected on his relationship with Teke. He was my best friend, he thought, as he began to choke up with sadness. Howard had rescued Teke who had been abandoned on the highway as a small puppy, and they had been together ever since. Teke had been there through his divorce, his mom's death, and all of medical school. He thought, Teke couldn't be dead! What will I do without him?

Still, he clung to a tiny doubt. Hoping against hope that Dr. Valentine had made an error, Howard pictured Teke wagging his tail when he reached him, and then they would go home and take a walk. He would be sure to let Dr. Valentine know he wasn't mad at him; the best doctors sometimes make mistakes.

When they got to the surgery area of the hospital, Howard saw Teke lying on the warm blanket that the staff had put under him. He did not wag his tail as Howard had hoped, but lay on his side with his eyes closed. His ball was beside him.

"We saved this for you," Dr. Valentine said, "in case you want to keep it. It was lodged in his throat, too deep for us to get it out in time. His airways were blocked. I know it's hard to imagine, but it was a peaceful death."

Howard was stunned. Just this morning they had enjoyed their morning walk before hospital rounds. Teke had taken his ball with him, carrying it in his mouth. He was a large German shepherd and people always stopped to comment on how beautiful and friendly he was. In fact, Howard had met a lot of people through Teke, especially at the dog park, where he took him as often as possible.

When Teke had started coughing and showing signs of distress, Howard had taken him to the veterinarian right away. A flood of thoughts and emotions fought for attention in Howard's mind. How could he not have noticed that Teke had swallowed his ball? If he had been paying closer attention, this wouldn't have happened. "It's my fault," Howard said quietly.

Howard could feel a lump forming in his throat, and tears beginning to well up in his eyes. I can't cry, he thought. It would look stupid, what with me being a doctor and all. After all, Teke was just a dog. Still, he couldn't help it. There was his best friend lying there, motionless, and there was no point in denying it any further.

Teke was gone.

"What would you like us to do with the body?" Dr. Valentine asked.

"What do you mean?" asked Howard. "What do you usually do?" Howard had no idea how to answer the question, since in his practice he had never had to ask that question.

"We can keep it here, or you can have a person from a pet memorial park pick it up, and then you can bury or cremate Teke. You can also take him home if you want to."

Howard began to get angry. How much did they expect of him? It was bad enough that they couldn't save Teke, now they wanted him to make a decision about the body. "And I thought human medicine was hard," Howard said.

If you have ever loved and lost a companion animal, you probably have a good idea of what Howard was feeling when he learned his beloved Teke was gone. In this chapter we'll examine the power of grief, taking it step by step, so that you can better understand the grieving process and how each stage can bring new and different feelings with it.

With pet loss, sometimes a sense of guilt is added to the typical stages of grief. Howard started feeling guilty just as soon as he discovered the cause of Teke's death. In fact, guilt may be the most difficult emotion that pet guardians must manage. There are so many circumstances where guilt about a companion animal's loss comes into play that we have devoted all of chapter 4 to this issue. But in this chapter let's look at grief itself, the phases of the grieving process, and some things that you can do to help yourself.

What Is Grief?

Grief is defined as the emotions and behavior that ensue when a love relationship has ended. When a loving human-animal bond is broken by the death of a companion animal, many surviving guardians will suffer a grieving period as intense as that they would feel if the departed loved one were a human being. (You might want to refer to your PAW score at this time to predict how you might respond to your own loss.)

It is important to remember that there is no right way to grieve. On some days you might feel pretty good and perhaps not think about your pet at all. Other days, however, you might find it difficult to think of anything else. Some people become numb and worry that they are not grieving enough. Again, remember there is no right or wrong way to grieve or to say good-bye. We all do it in our own time.

Let's look at some of the most common symptoms of grief. You might be surprised to learn that there are so many signs, and you may have even mistaken some of them for something other than grief.

o   Crying

o   Numbness

o   Fatigue

o   Depression

o   Loneliness

o   Difficulty eating or sleeping

o   Sadness

o   Denial

o   Meaningful dreams about your beloved pet

o   Shock

o   Confusion

o   Aching

o   Blaming

o   Irritability

o   Anxiety

o   Withdrawal

o   Relief

o   Inability to concentrate

o   Guilt

o   Sighing and crying

Do any of these symptoms describe what you are feeling? If so, let's see what you can do to help yourself navigate through the stages of grieving.

Tools to Help You Through Your Grief

1. You might want to take a moment to identify how many of the signs of grief you currently have. For each symptom, assign it a score from 1 (low) to 5 (high). Also, are there emotions or behaviors you are feeling or doing that aren't on the list? If so, write them down, as well, and assign each a score. Once a week, refer to your list and give new scores to the signs of grief as they fade. This will help you to record and note your own progress in recovering from this painful experience.

2. Get out of the house, even if it's just a quick stroll to the mailbox, a trip to the grocery store, or a walk around the block.

3. Exercise. No matter how much time you spend exercising, even if it's only for a few minutes each day, it will help you feel better emotionally as well as physically.

4. Eat well, but don't over- or undereat.

5. If you have trouble sleeping, get up after twenty minutes of trying to fall asleep. Go into another room and do something else. Watch television, read a book, play on the Internet, or listen to music. When you begin to feel sleepy, return to your bed. You don't want to associate your bed with negative or sad emotions. This will only make it harder for you to sleep in the future.

6. Meditate or take a mindfulness walk.

7. Break the routine you had with your pet. For example, if you walked your dog at 6:00 every evening, it might help to purposely choose a different activity for that time.

8. Schedule time for your grief. Spend a certain amount of time each day thinking about your loss. Time it. It could be five minutes or thirty minutes. After the time is up, consciously think of something else, preferably something pleasant and not related to your companion animal. It's very difficult, if not impossible, for the mind to think of two things at the same time. Remember, you are not betraying your love for your pet by not staying in pain twenty-four hours a day. You might ask yourself if your pet would want you to suffer so much. The answer would undoubtedly be "no."

9. Talk to someone who understands your loss, or attend a pet-loss support group, or both.

10. Talk and write about what you miss. For example, what has knowing this being brought into your life? What have you learned from your companion animal?

11. Accept the grief. Roll with its tides. Don't try to be brave. Grief hurts.

12. Postpone making major decisions. For example, wait before you decide to quit your job, sell your house, or move.

13. Find a way to help others. If you have writing ability, use it. Much great literature has been written as tributes to someone loved and lost.

14. For the time being, put away remembrances of your pet, such as pictures, blankets, toys, or other reminders that may upset you. If you choose to, bring them out slowly as you begin to feel better.

15. Avoid substance abuse, especially prescription or nonprescription medications. This also includes alcohol, tobacco, and caffeine.

The Phases of Grieving

In her pioneering work, *On Death and Dying* (1963), Elisabeth Kubler-Ross described the following five stages that characterize the grieving process:

1. Denial

2. Anger

3. Bargaining

4. Depression

5. Acceptance

It is important to note that the process is not linear. In other words, once you've gotten through the anger phase and moved on to depression, you will probably at some time come back to anger or even to denial. Knowing this, perhaps you will not become as frustrated as you might if your grief does not follow a straight line, beginning with denial, and proceeding systematically through anger, bargaining, depression, and ending with acceptance.

Denial (or Disbelief)

Upon receiving the telegram that informed him of his daughter's death, Mark Twain (1924) wrote: "It is one of the mysteries of our nature that a man, all unprepared, can receive a thunderstroke like this and live. There is but one explanation of it. The intellect is stunned by the shock and but gropingly gathers the meaning of the words. The power to realize their full import is mercifully wanting."

For most of us, the death of our companion animals is a shock that is hard to understand and accept, just as Twain's loss of his daughter was. But the psyche goes into survival mode and protects us from having to immediately absorb and cope with the loss and its implications. The psyche activates a protective psychological mechanism known as *denial*. As Twain so eloquently pointed out, sometimes it is merciful to have this protection.

Remember Howard, in the story at the beginning of this chapter? He couldn't believe Teke was dead, even though he was a physician and an intelligent person. On the one hand, he knew that there was no mix-up and that Dr. Valentine most likely had not made a mistake. On the other hand, he had to see Teke's lifeless body for himself. He couldn't believe in Teke's passing unless he saw it for himself.

You can think of denial as a sort of time-release cold capsule. Time-release pills deliver medication slowly, over a period of time, so the body can absorb it more easily. Denial works in much the same way. A sudden onslaught of traumatic psychological pain actually can make us physically ill, or even send us into a major depression. In spite of the general perception that denial is an unhealthy state of mind, it actually is a normal response and perhaps even a healthy way of coping with a terrible loss gradually.

Here's an example. A colleague of mine lost his teenaged daughter in a tragic accident while she was traveling abroad. He was devastated upon hearing the news, but he still was able to function and perform the tasks he needed to. He had to notify friends and family, arrange to have her body shipped home, plan a funeral—he even delivered a eulogy at her memorial service—and attend to dozens of other logistical details.

A few weeks after his daughter's funeral, my colleague admitted that the only reason he could accomplish these tasks was that he was in a state of disbelief. "Even though on the surface I acknowledged the fact of her death," he said, "had the *reality* of it sunk in immediately, I would have been paralyzed with grief and unable to do the things that needed to be done. I moved on autopilot, thinking the whole time that it was a terrible mistake and my daughter was still alive and well."

For many of us, there is an aspect of unreality about death. Because of this, we may deny that it has happened. This is especially true if the death was unexpected or sudden, but denial also can occur when the end has been anticipated. Many people think that if they know that their pet is dying, they can prepare themselves for the loss; in other words, they believe that they can grieve beforehand, and the grief will not be as intense after the actual loss. After working with hundreds of people over the years it seems to me that this rarely happens.

We can never really know how we are going to respond to the loss, although, certainly, obtaining information and education about grief beforehand, in anticipation of it hitting us, can help. Unfortunately, no amount of information or education will alleviate the pain you will most likely suffer when your friend is no longer with you.

You may also think you see or hear your companion animal within the first weeks of your loss. A number of people have called me and said that this has happened to them, and they are afraid they are losing their minds, because only "crazy" people see and hear things. One woman told me that after her cat, Alex, died, she heard him meow almost every night, just before she fell asleep. It was so real that she got out of bed to look around the house for him, even though she knew he was gone. She was not going crazy, and neither are you! Remember, you are in a state of disbelief. Your psyche is used to hearing and seeing your pet, so, for a while, it may believe that your pet is still here. If this continues for more than a few months, however, you may want to consult a mental health professional.

Denial and Missing Pets

If your pet is missing and you have no confirmation it is actually dead, the denial stage can be lengthier. If this is the case for you, it may help you to understand that gaining closure in this first stage of the grieving process is indeed hard. It's especially difficult for you to believe your companion animal is really gone because, in the absence of concrete proof, you may be clinging to a tiny hope for a miracle.

Families of combat soldiers who are classified "missing in action" experience the same reaction. Even though they understand intellectually that their loved one is most likely dead, emotionally they have a lot of trouble accepting the truth. What about all those stories of missing pets who travel thousands of miles to reunite with their guardians? Because of these miraculous stories, you may feel guilty about abandoning hope that your missing companion animal simply might turn up one day. It may help you to know that, if your pet is gone for more than a week, there's a high probability that he or she won't be coming back. This statistical evidence might be enough to help move you out of denial and through the rest of the stages of grieving.

Of course, this doesn't mean that you shouldn't look for your friend. Posting signs and flyers and checking animal shelters should be an immediate priority as soon as your pet disappears. (Note: Just in case your companion animal's identification comes loose and falls off, a microchip inserted under your pet's skin is a great way for animal control, your local humane society, or your veterinarian to locate you and let you know that your pet has been found. It is also insurance that you are the actual guardian. Check with your veterinarian about the possibility of microchipping.)

Tools to Help You Through Denial

1. Commemorate your pet's death. For example, you can hold a funeral or a memorial service. Remember, funerals for human beings are not for those who have died, but for the living. A farewell service is a way to break through your denial. There are pet cemeteries in most cities, or your veterinarian can handle the body for you. You can have your beloved cremated and keep the ashes, or perhaps scatter them someplace that your pet loved. You don't need ashes or a body to commemorate your pet, however. Even a simple moment of thanks for the gift you were given can be a form of commemoration.

2. If your companion had fur, cut off a bit of his or her fur and put it in a special place, perhaps a locket or a pretty box. You can still feel the softness, even if you can't pet the living being.

3. Be gentle with yourself. Healing takes time, so allow yourself to stay in denial as long as you need to be, especially if your pet is missing rather than confirmed dead. Your psyche will let you know when it's time to move to the next phase of the grieving process.

Bargaining

After hearing an unfavorable medical diagnosis about their companion animal, many people begin a bargaining process, usually with whatever they consider a Higher Power than themselves. For example, you might say, "I'll go to church every Sunday if *you* just let Snoopy live." Or, "If *you* just help Sam to get better, I'll take him to the dog park every day." It's natural to wish or pray for your pet to be well and stay with you. Moreover, it probably makes people feel better if they throw in a personal sacrifice or two to help cement the deal.

Despite your best intentions and most fervent promises, however, bargains don't really work.

Tools for Bargaining

I wish there were an effective tool to deal with the bargaining stage of grief. There isn't. Probably the best thing you can do is to be aware that no matter how much you offer, or how hard you bargain, it doesn't really work. Even knowing this, though, it may feel right to you to try to bargain anyway. If this is the case, go ahead and bargain away. There are no rules for dealing with the stages of grief and it is smart to do whatever makes you feel better.

Anger

When you finally believe that your beloved pet is dead or you truly understand that he or she is going to die, you might find yourself getting angry. This anger may be unjustly directed at innocent people. The cause of this misdirected anger is that you may not be totally realistic at this particular time. You are in pain, and it seems as if it should be someone's fault. You may want to express your anger by casting blame.

The following list shows the most common targets that pet guardians choose to direct their anger against:

1. Themselves

2. The animal

3. Others involved in the animal's loss, i.e., the veterinarian, veterinary staff, the person who may have run over the pet, etc.

4. Other pet owners whose pets are still alive

5. God

You may ask yourself many unanswerable questions: Why did my pet have to die? Why didn't the veterinarian do more? Why didn't I go to the veterinarian sooner? Why me?

Because there are no answers to the questions you may have, you may find yourself becoming even angrier and more frustrated. It may be helpful to understand that the animal or person who angers you was probably unaware of or unable to control the situation. Remember how angry Howard became with Dr. Valentine when he asked how Howard wanted to deal with Teke's body? Dr. Valentine needed to know what Howard's wishes were, but Howard thought he was demanding too much from him, and he felt extreme anger. This is very common, and veterinarians are familiar with this response.

It's good to know this, so when you become less angry, you will realize that the entire veterinary hospital staff understands your anger as a normal part of your grieving process. Knowing this will also make it easier to see the veterinarian again if you should get another companion animal in the future.

Tools to Help You Through Your Anger

1. Recognize that anger is often a mask for hurt or fear rather than real anger. When you get angry with someone during this stage of the process, you might ask yourself, "Am I really mad at this person, or am I just afraid I can't cope with the loss of my companion?" In either case, take some slow, deep, even breaths, and give yourself a chance to think clearly and reasonably.

2. When angry, ask yourself, "Am I being reasonable or unreasonable?" For example, do you have a suspicion that the veterinarian purposely killed your dog in surgery because he doesn't like pit bulls? If you have substantial reason to believe the veterinarian intentionally killed your pet, get more information to discover whether your belief is warranted. If it is, you should report him or her to your state veterinary licensing board. It would be more likely, however, that your suspicion is unreasonable and is caused solely by the anger you feel over your loss. It will take some conscious effort, but try to change your thinking to reflect what truly happened. You'll probably notice that when you change your thinking, your anger will soften and your pain will deepen. The pain, however, will be a truer reflection of how you actually feel.

3. Get as much physical exercise as possible.

4. Scream! If you are really angry, screaming can help you to release your anger without hurting yourself or anyone else. If you don't have a place where you can scream without attracting attention, try screaming in your car, with the windows rolled up. (Caution: Don't do this while you're actually driving; wait

until you are parked somewhere. Should others see you, they will probably think you're singing along with the radio.)

5. If screaming is not your style and you want to release the anger that you feel seething within yourself, hit a pillow, or take a baseball bat or tennis racket and hit the bed.

6. Talk to your veterinarian about any concerns you have. Ask these or any other questions you might have: Could I have done more? Are resources available to help me? What would you have done?

Guilt

In addition to episodes of anger, you may feel guilty. It is not uncommon for people to feel that they were responsible for their pet's death. In fact, guilt is perhaps the most easily distinguishable difference between grief over the loss of a human being and grief over the loss of a companion animal, especially if you have euthanized your pet.

But because our companion animals depend on us for all of their medical decisions, we sometimes must opt for this choice. For me, it is the last humane thing I can do for my beloved pet; nevertheless, it is never an easy decision. The next chapter is devoted to this aspect of loss, as well as to other issues that you may feel guilty about regarding the loss of your pet.

Depression

Depression is the time when our emotions lessen in intensity and settle into one sorrowful expression. Most people experiencing depression feel a lack of motivation to do much of anything. If possible, they try to withdraw from what they see as a busy, happy world. "After all, everyone else is happy but me, right?" is a common thought.

Another common symptom of depression has been called the "pangs of grief." Your pet is missed, and you undergo periods of anxiety, crying, helplessness, hopelessness, powerlessness, and a general lack of interest in your surroundings and daily activities. These grief pangs usually begin within a few hours or days of your loss and usually reach their peak of severity within fourteen days.

Remember, however, that one size does not fit all. You may experience pangs of grief that last much longer than two weeks, or you may not experience any. There is no "normal" template for the stages of grieving. Just as every human being is both alike and different, so too is the grieving process. It has commonalties and differences for every person's situation. Your depression may be worse if your companion was a big part of your social life, or if he or she was your best friend.

Howard met many of his friends by taking Teke to the dog park, much as a parent takes a child to the playground and makes friends with the other parents there. When you no longer have your dog, these people may disappear from your life, leaving you feeling even more alone and isolated.

Moreover, if your pet was your best friend, your pain is every bit as great as if your pet had been a human being. Think of all the life transitions Howard went through, with Teke always by his side. The memories of the life experiences you shared with your pet may come flooding back to you, and you may find yourself grieving anew for earlier sorrows lost in the past.

Some people stay depressed for a long time, others for shorter periods. Common symptoms of depression include the following:

1. Depressed mood most of the day, nearly every day

2. Markedly diminished interest or pleasure in all, or almost all, activities that were formerly pleasurable

3. Significant weight loss or gain

4. Insomnia

5. Feelings of agitation or restlessness

6. Fatigue or loss of energy

7. Feelings of worthlessness or inappropriate guilt

8. Diminished ability to think or concentrate, or indecisiveness

9. Recurrent thoughts of death, recurrent thoughts of suicide

If you experience five or more of these symptoms during the same two-week period, you may have a more serious depression than would normally be expected with the loss of a companion animal. Sometimes, the loss of our beloved pets can trigger other unresolved losses and leave us feeling so overwhelmed that even suicide seems like a good option.

If you feel suicidal, please get the help that is available to you. Reading this book and doing the exercises, while beneficial, may not be enough. If suicide lingers in your mind for any length of time, consulting a mental health professional would be a better option.

If you do seek professional help to get the guidance you need during this difficult time, be sure to let the therapist know that you have lost a pet, and explain the importance of that pet in your life. Many therapists are not well educated about the intensity of grief that the loss of a companion animal can trigger, and they may not ask you directly if this is a factor in your current emotional turmoil.

A popular television show called *Judging Amy* features a character named Maxine, played by actress Tyne Daly. In one episode, Maxine was having a day overflowing with stress, both personal and professional, when she discovered her dog, Socrates, dead under a tree. Because she had so many other issues to deal with, she didn't react at all to the loss of Socrates and simply went about her day.

Finally, all the pressure she was under got to be too much for her, and she went to see a therapist. After some initial probing, the therapist finally asked Maxine bluntly, "Why are you here?" Maxine said, "My dog died," and burst into tears. Of all the pressures Maxine was enduring, that was the one that had affected her the most profoundly. The therapist might never have asked her directly whether she had lost a pet, so it was valuable for the therapeutic process when Maxine revealed her sad news. The therapist needed that information to provide guidance.

Tools to Help You Through Your Depression

1. Recognize the symptoms of depression.

2. Talk or cry with sympathetic and knowledgeable people.

3. Stay as active as you can.

4. Remember that others who loved your companion animal may also be experiencing the same feelings. They also may experience them at different times.

5. Laugh. Remember that your companion was a great humor therapist, so allow him or her to help you through this difficult time. Think of some things that your pet did that made you laugh, and, if you have to, force yourself to at least smile at the memory of some of these antics. I'll bet you can think of many.

6. Try to stay away from black-and-white thinking. For example, you might find yourself saying, "I'll *never* get over this," or "Something sad *always* seems to happen to me but not to others." When you hear yourself speaking or thinking in these absolute terms—"never," "always"—change your language to

more accurate reflections such as, "It's hard getting over this, but I know I will," or, "Sometimes sad things happen to me, but I also experience happiness just as others do."

Even if you experience depression and it passes after a reasonable time, it may recur during times that had special meaning for you and your pet. Did Snowball like to bat around the Christmas ornaments while you decorated the tree? Did Duke make it an annual ritual to bounce along joyfully with the kids when they hunted for Easter eggs? Memories like these can trigger sadness in you when these special days arrive, and your companion animal isn't around to be part of the celebration. Don't be surprised if depression returns.

It might help you to get through these times by changing your routine a bit. Invite a crowd of friends and family members to help you decorate for Christmas. Include a special tribute to your pet in your Hanukkah celebration. Tell those close to you about how big a part of those special times your companion used to be; share a laugh over a happy memory.

Acceptance

You will know when you have accepted your loss because you will begin to smile again. You'll take a fresh look at the world around you and remember the happy times you had with your companion animal. There will be no heart-wrenching pain, but instead, wonderful memories of the times you had together. You will find you have the emotional energy to reinvest in a new way of being, ready to latch on to something new, perhaps even a new pet.

Tools to Help You Accept Your Loss

1. This might be the time to bring out pictures of your pet. Display them on your mantel, or place a picture on the table beside your companion's favorite napping chair. Once you have reached the acceptance phase, photos will bring you comfort and happy memories instead of triggering sadness and tears.

2. Think about getting a new pet. As hard as it is to get through the loss of a beloved companion, by now you've probably reached the point where the joy your companion brought to you becomes more prominent in your memory than the pain of the loss. A new pet will add many joyful times to your life. You will also be helping another animal have a wonderful home.

Homes with Several Pets

Many pet guardians have more than one companion animal. If this is the case in your home, you may be wondering how you can help your remaining pet or pets to get through this difficult time. After all, pets form emotional connections with one another, as well as with their human friends, and the loss of one is sure to have an effect on the others. Sensitive pet guardians know that they need to pay special attention to their remaining pets, even while dealing with their own emotional pain.

Cathy and Joey

Cathy came to my office one day. She had just lost her three-year-old dachshund, Joey, to cancer. When Joey was just a year old, Cathy and her husband had adopted two more dachshund puppies, Jamie and Samie. Joey soon became the puppies' whole world. They slept with him, ate with him, and generally looked to him for clues on how to be a dog. They barked when he barked, played with the same toys he played with, and followed him everywhere. Cathy took all three on walks together and to the dog park at least once a week.

When Joey became sick, Cathy cared for him as lovingly as any mother could care for her child. Cathy and her husband had no children, so she thought of all three of them as her animal children. Joey's illness and the care he required intensified the bond Cathy had with him, and when he died, her grief was acute, sharp and agonizing.

She also recognized that Jamie and Samie were having difficulties with the loss of their friend. Before Joey died, they had loved to go for rides in the car; now they trembled and whimpered whenever Cathy took them anywhere in the car. She didn't know what to do for them and asked if I had any suggestions.

Fortunately, I have a friend who is both a veterinarian and animal behaviorist, so I called him for help. He confirmed that when one animal dies in a multiple-animal household, things change for everyone, including the remaining animal or animals. Much as in a family when one child leaves home, a new configuration evolves, and new roles are established. For example, the second-oldest child often will move into the older sibling's room.

Jamie and Samie were used to having Joey as their leader, he was their "alpha" dog; and they had become accustomed to life with Joey always present. With Joey gone, they became confused about how to act and what to do.

The animal behaviorist told Cathy that when she took the dogs in the car, instead of saying "It's okay" and comforting them, as she had been doing, it would be better to ignore their whimpering. Instead, when they reached their destination, she was instructed to reward them with a treat for any positive behavior. We know that in dealing with children we have more success getting desired results by ignoring negative behavior and rewarding the positive. So, too, is it with animals.

Cathy learned that her situation was almost like having two new puppies and that she was, in some ways, starting over with their training. She began choosing a different route for their walks (which helped her, too, because she was not so frequently reminded of Joey). She gave Jamie and Samie new toys, a new bed, and she took them to new and different places, and with the passage of time, Jamie and Samie and Cathy recovered from their loss.

If you are trying to help a surviving pet or pets to establish a new role, remember to reward positive behaviors and, as much as possible, ignore negative ones. Remember, too, that animals can often sense when their guardian is upset, anxious, or sad. So some of their behaviors may not be signs of grief over the deceased pet but, actually, a response to your own grief. If anxious behaviors do get out of control, though, it is wise to seek the help of an animal behaviorist. Usually, however, with time and patience, a new social grouping will be established, and both animals and pet guardians will fall into the new rhythms and dynamics of a different family unit.

How Well Are You Handling Your Pet's Death?

Please write a "Y" or an "N" ("yes" or "no") at the end of each question as your answer. At the end, count up all the "Y" answers, with one point earned for each "yes."

1. Do you wish that you were reacting differently, emotionally and mentally, to the death of your pet? ____

2. Are you bothered by other people's reactions? ____

3. Do you feel your life has lost its meaning, but don't know what to do to fill the void? ____

4. Do you feel you could have taken better care of your pet?
____

5. Are you feeling apathetic, and just can't seem to face your pet's death? _____

6. Are you crying and upset too much of the time? Do you feel that you are overreacting emotionally? _____

7. Are you tuning out and avoiding facing your feelings because you are afraid that they will be too overwhelming to handle? _____

8. Are you reluctant to get another pet because you fear that one day it, too, will be gone? _____

9. Are you depressed? _____

10. Do you have difficulty finding good, empathetic, and supportive friends or groups? _____

11. Are you uncertain what the loss of your pet actually means to your life? _____

12. Are you having trouble finding what to say to your children about the death of the family pet? _____

13. Are you feeling conflicted about a decision to euthanize your pet? _____

14. Are you undecided whether to be present during euthanasia? _____

15. Are you uncertain about when is the right time to get another pet? _____

16. Do you wish your family were more supportive and understanding about your loss? _____

Write the total here: _____

o   If you scored 9–16, your loss has greatly affected you. You may want to develop more knowledge and understanding about the stages of grieving, and use the tools that can help you with coping, such as the tools in this book. A pet-loss support group or talking to a mental health professional may also be helpful.

o   If you scored 6–9, you fluctuate between handling your loss effectively and not handling your loss well at all. You are partially on the right path, but you need some guidance on dealing with the emotional hazards you are now encountering.

o   If you scored 1–3, you are handling the bereavement process well. You will be noticing your signs of recovery shortly.

Reprinted with permission from Diane Kelley, Ph.D., Los Angeles, CA (310) 559-3164

In this chapter, we have just briefly touched upon the subject of guilt and its place in the grieving process. But if you have lost a companion animal, you may find that guilt is predominant throughout every stage of grief that you experience. Guilt's destructive power is often underestimated. In the next chapter we will examine this emotion in greater detail. You will come face to face with guilt, understand it, and learn how to deal with it effectively.

Chapter 4

Drowning in Guilt

You can't always control circumstances, but you can control your own thoughts.

—Charles Popplestone

Virginia cried as she said, "If only I had had more money, I could have saved him. It's not fair that the rich can buy all the help they need, and I couldn't save Charlie because I couldn't afford the treatment for him. I feel so guilty. I should have been able to find the money for him somehow." And she burst into tears again. Charlie had been Virginia's longtime companion and friend, a black-and-white cocker spaniel whose life had ended because of cancer, and she was wracked with guilt over not being able to save him.

As you will soon learn (if you don't know it already), guilt is a common and powerful response to pet loss. We discussed the issue of guilt briefly in chapter 3, but now we will examine it in detail. If you're like most people, you may have experienced or even currently be feeling some guilt over the loss of a companion animal. In fact, you might be surprised to learn that pet guardians often feel more guilt over the loss of a companion animal than the loss of a loved human. In the pet-loss groups that I run, I frequently hear expressions of guilt much like Virginia's, who told her story at a recent group meeting.

The Face of Guilt

In the same pet-loss group, Sarah told a story that was quite different. She had come home late the evening before, having accidentally left the latch to her front door open. Her inquisitive and fearless feline, Sam, had taken the opportunity to let himself out for the evening. Sarah lived in an area near a canyon that sheltered a variety of wildlife, and Sam, who was usually an indoor cat, was not aware of the wily coyotes who preyed on small animals including domestic felines. He had been no match for a coyote.

Sarah said, "I can never forgive myself. If only I had latched the door, Sam would still be here with me. What am I going to tell my friends? I feel guilty and embarrassed. They're going to think I killed him by my stupidity. And I guess I did."

Carol was the last person to speak. She said, "I killed my dog yesterday." Someone in the group asked what had happened. "He was sixteen and too sick to save, so I euthanized him. To me, it's the same as killing him, though the veterinarian assured me it was the best decision since Zeke was in so much pain. But did I have the right to take his life? Shouldn't that be God's decision?"

The members of the group sat quietly. They had no answer for Carol. But the meeting room was almost humming with deeply felt emotions. There was crying, anger, and sadness, but even beyond these emotions, all three group members expressed deep guilt. All three felt that they had done something wrong, and that they were guilty of killing the dear friends that they had nurtured, loved, and given the best homes that any companion animal could hope for.

In all of my years of facilitating pet-loss support groups, I've observed that guilt is the biggest hurdle for people to handle. There is no real comparison with the loss of loved humans, because we do not euthanize human beings, and it's relatively rare for them to end their lives accidentally. That is why this entire chapter is devoted to the issue of guilt. Guilt is very common and very persistent in the grieving process, especially when grieving for the loss of a companion animal.

What Is Guilt?

In its simplest definition, *guilt* is a thought triggered by a past event. It is a very normal response to the perception that, somehow, we have failed our companion animals. These thoughts of guilt evoke feelings of remorse, shame, anxiety, anger, and sadness. We ask ourselves questions like, Why did I do what I did? Why didn't I get my pet to the veterinarian sooner? Why couldn't I have done more? Did I euthanize him/her too soon or too late? Did I have an incompetent veterinarian? Did I have the right to play God? No matter what the circumstances of their pet's death, most people feel some degree of guilt if they have chosen to euthanize their companion animal, even more so if they have killed it accidentally.

Think about the three people in the pet-loss group at the beginning of this chapter. All of them believed that they should have done something differently. Virginia thought that if she had somehow found the money for further treatments, her companion would still be alive. This may or may not have been true, but she erred on the side of blaming herself. Sarah lost her pet because of her own accidental carelessness, and she felt both shame and anger with herself, completely ignoring the fact that she would never have killed her pet *intentionally*. Carol, on the other hand, had deliberately euthanized her best friend, and then wondered if she had done the right thing, even though her pet was old and in pain, and the veterinarians had assured her she was making the right decision.

Very few people ever feel it's the right time to lose their pet. Unfortunately, our companion animals do not usually live as long as we do, so most of us will have to go through the grief of losing some of them at some point in our lives. Many people would say that the ideal death for their pet would be to have it die in their arms, peacefully and comfortably. As wonderful as this ideal might be, it rarely happens, and we are often faced with the necessity to make decisions for our companions that we would rather not make.

Knowing that guilt is a normal part of the grieving process might make it a little easier to bear. It's human to dwell on the "what ifs" and "shoulds." In fact, guilt is such a common human response that psychiatrist Karen Horney (1950) put a label to this concept, calling it "the tyranny of the shoulds." Horney suggested that most people were "split" into two selves, which she called the "despised self" and the "ideal self." To understand this concept, you could think of your ideal self as something you create out of all the "shoulds" that you think would turn you into a perfect, or an ideal, person. Unfortunately, creating an ideal self is both unrealistic and, ultimately, impossible.

Trying to be perfect can lead only to frustration and self-blame. This is how we create a despised self, composed of all our perceived failings. Sometimes, we convince ourselves that we can control the random hazards of existence, even when, realistically, we know that we cannot. It would be much healthier to accept ourselves as "human," and therefore imperfect, and do the best we can, not allowing the "shoulds" to take over our lives and keep us from healing.

Can you see how this concept applies to guilty thoughts over pet loss? Somehow, we convince ourselves that the perfect person should have been more in charge and able to save the beloved companion. When that didn't happen, we assume that the despised self, the one who is irresponsible, not wealthy enough, or who gives up too easily was in charge and made the wrong decisions. It's no wonder guilt is so common when our pets die. If you find yourself using the word "should" a lot, you might want to consider reading more of Dr. Horney's work. (Suggested reading can be found in the back of the book.)

The next section discusses the origins of guilt, so that you will gain an even better understanding of why most of us feel guilty about the loss of our companion animals. Before reading further, however, you might want to try the following activities. You also might want to get out your journal or tape recorder before you begin.

Activity: Taking a Look at Yourself

1. Read again the stories of the different pet-loss situations at the beginning of this chapter. Do you identify with any of the people in the support group? Do you identify with any of their stories? If so, perhaps you might want to write or talk about your

thoughts and feelings in regard to the support group's stories. What would you tell the different group members if you were their friend, counselor, or relative. Then, if what you would tell them differs from what you have told yourself, ask yourself, how and why?

2. If your story is different from those at the beginning of the chapter, write it down, and then ask yourself how you would respond if you heard your story from another person. Would you condemn that person, or would you show compassion? What you can learn from this exercise is this: If you can show compassion to someone else, perhaps you can ease up a bit on yourself. After all, no matter what your situation, at the time, you did do the best that you could do.

3. Pay attention to the words that you use. If you hear yourself saying, "I should have" or "If only," or if you're beating yourself up with words, generally, stop it, and ask yourself if this is really a "should." Maybe it is your ideal self blaming you for things that you had no control over. If this is the case, make a conscious effort to change your thinking. Say out loud to yourself something like, "I did the best that I could," or "I gave Tara the best home she could have had. It is not my fault that I cannot control all of the events in my life or my pet's life."

The Origins of Guilt

Have you ever wondered why you feel guilty? The origins of guilt, or the lack thereof, usually can be traced back to what we learned as children. Parents, teachers, and clergy all tried to teach us what they consider right or wrong. Guilty thoughts arise if we violate an internal moral norm that we have been taught to accept as valid. A person who feels guilty, notes philosopher Herbert Morris (1971), is one who has internalized, or accepted, the moral norms and, as such, is committed to not violating them.

Unfortunately, the issue gets a little cloudy when a "wrong" has been committed accidentally. Even if no intentional harm was committed, the resulting guilt is just as strong as if the harm had been deliberate. This is especially true if you feel that you have somehow participated in or contributed to the loss of your companion animal.

Do these phrases sound familiar to you?

o If only I had been more careful.

o   If only I had paid more attention.

o   If only I had seen the signs of illness.

If you can force yourself, it may help you to think differently. For example, if you are learning from your past and trying to avoid repeating errors, accidental or intentional, then guilt is useless. Guilt is not merely a concern with the past, guilt is an immobilization in the present about a past event. In other words, you get stuck.

If you're not able to learn from the past and move forward, the degree of being stuck can range from mild upset to severe depression. Learning from your mistakes is a healthy and necessary part of growth. Guilt is unhealthy because when you are feeling guilty, you are ineffectively focusing your present energy on the past. Moreover, as everyone knows, you cannot change the past.

There are some psychological reasons for choosing guilt, none of which is particularly healthy, but people choose these reasons all the time. As you read through the following list, think about whether any apply to you, and think about how you are currently feeling about the loss of your pet, or about any issue with which you might be struggling. If some of these sound familiar, you might want to work on changing your thoughts.

1. By using the present to feel guilty about the past, you do not have to act in any kind of effective, self-enhancing way. Thus, guilt becomes an avoidance technique for not working on yourself.

2. There is a tendency to believe that if you feel guilty enough, eventually, you will be forgiven.

3. Sometimes, you can win approval of others by showing that you feel guilty.

4. By shifting responsibility backward, for example, the choices you may have made about your pet's care, you not only avoid the hard work of changing yourself now, but the risks and opportunity that go with change, too.

Strategies for Eliminating Guilt

Guilt, like all self-defeating thoughts, is a choice. It is something that you can exercise control over. It takes effort, but if you choose to, you can work through it. Here are some ways to eliminate guilt from your thinking:

1. Accept the past, no matter how you feel about it. Tell yourself, "My guilty thoughts will not change the past."

2. Ask yourself what you are avoiding in the present by feeling guilty about the past. By working on this issue, you may eliminate your guilt.

3. When guilty thoughts come to mind, disrupt them by telling yourself to stop thinking those thoughts. Say **STOP**, firmly, out loud if you need to. Replace it with a more positive thought such as, "I did the best I could."

4. Ask what it would it take to forgive yourself. Can you begin doing it? Say out loud, "I forgive myself." Say it several times each day.

5. Remember the good things you did in the relationship with your pet and all of the loving care you gave. Write those things down and refer to them when guilty thoughts arise.

6. If possible, participate in a pet-loss support group. It's a powerful way to obtain forgiveness from others and to give forgiveness to others who also might be in need.

The 90/10 Secret

The 90/10 secret is a simple fact of life that we need to remind ourselves of every day. Very few people are consciously aware of this secret, and some of those who are aware of it refuse to believe it. The result? Millions needlessly suffer undeserved stress, trials, and heartache. Bad days follow bad days. Guilt continues.

What is this life-altering secret? Here it is:

o *Ten percent of life is made up of what happens to you.*

o *Ninety percent of life is determined by how you react to what happens to you.*

What does this mean? We really have no control over 10 percent of what happens to us. We cannot stop our car from wearing out. We cannot control a malignant tumor that won't respond to chemotherapy. We can't control a driver who seemingly comes out of nowhere and hits our cat. These are events that we simply cannot influence, no matter how much we might like to think we can. But think about it: These events make up only 10 percent of our lives. That's a very small percentage over an entire lifetime.

The other 90 percent is different. You determine the other 90 percent of your life by your reactions to the 10 percent. You cannot control the death of your pet, but you can control your reaction to it. This does not mean that feelings of grief aren't legitimate, normal, and healthy; guilt, however, is not. You can control your guilt by using some of the methods described in the previous section.

Perhaps you're thinking that you can't control your reactions to a situation. Reactions are instinctive and not governed by logical thought, right? Well, the good news is that you can indeed control your reactions, and when you learn how to do that, you will appreciate how helpful it will be in moving you through the grieving

Controlling and Changing Your Thoughts

Does it sound hard when you consider controlling or changing your thoughts? After all, thoughts and feelings just happen, don't they? How can you control them? It's not as difficult as you might think. You know, of course, that people are capable of being brainwashed. So, what is brainwashing? It is taking what a person thinks and changing it. Political regimes often use brainwashing on their citizens, or on the citizens of other countries. Perhaps you've heard of a radio service called Voice of America. It broadcasts the virtues of democracy into undemocratic countries, with the intent of helping the citizens of those countries to think differently about their living situations and their governments. The goal is to inspire action or an uprising that might ultimately bring about a democratic state. This is a form of brainwashing, or deliberately trying to change thoughts.

Have you ever noticed how often you can change your mind about a particular situation? The reason this happens is that you begin to think differently about something, perhaps because you've learned new information or perhaps because you've simply had time to think about it in a different way. This, in turn, allows you to feel differently.

For example, if I accidentally ran over my precious cat, I might think I was the most horrible pet guardian in the world and I would certainly feel guilt, anger, shame, and sadness. However, guilt is not a feeling. It is a thought. This concept is important because if I ask you to not feel sad, you may think I'm asking the impossible. However, if I ask you to think about why you "think" you are guilty, you might come up with some ideas.

Many pet guardians have told me they think that if they stop grieving, or stop having guilty thoughts, that must mean they didn't care enough. It's almost as if the memory of their departed pet would be gone if they stopped grieving or thinking they were guilty.

This might be the time to remember that you are not betraying your love for your pet by not staying in pain twenty-four hours a day You might ask yourself if your pet would want you to be feeling so much anguish. The answer would undoubtedly be "no."

Recently, I asked one of my clients if she thought that her dog would want her to be experiencing so much psychological pain. Her answer was, "No, I know Toes won't be at peace until I am at peace. That's why I want to feel better." I asked her if I could quote her answer in this book and she said, "Yes, it might actually help me and others realize that we can let the pain go, and still know we loved our pets."

Activity: Controlling and Changing Your Thoughts

Think of something that you believe you were guilty of doing regarding your companion animal. It doesn't have to involve loss. Perhaps you think you're guilty because you didn't pay enough attention to your pet. Take note of how this makes you feel: mad, sad, or afraid, or glad or relieved because your pet is no longer in pain. There may be more than one feeling associated with your guilt. Make a list of all of the thoughts you have regarding this situation. While you're making your list, try to keep the following instructions in mind:

1. Pay attention to the positives.

2. Don't exaggerate the negatives.

3. Be careful not to overgeneralize.

If you notice that your thoughts are irrational, try to change them to a more rational mode. For example, here's an irrational thought: "I ran over my cat, so I must be the world's worst pet guardian. I shouldn't be allowed to even have a pet."

Now let's turn that thought into a rational one: "It is not possible for me to be the world's worst pet guardian. Someone has to be worse than I. Of course, I should be allowed to have pets, I care for them deeply."

After you complete this exercise and turn irrational thoughts into rational ones, see if your feelings have changed or perhaps shifted.

Rational Emotive Behavioral Therapy

Albert Ellis was one of the first psychologists to write about the idea that thoughts come before feelings (1985). His theory, called Rational Emotive Behavioral Therapy, is one of the best tools for changing belief systems and, ultimately, feelings. The theory can be of great use to you as you work through your guilty thoughts.

Rational Emotive Behavioral Therapy begins with the ABC's.

A stands for the *Activating Event*: in other words, something has happened. Since this is a book about pet loss, let's look at Ellis's work from the perspective of losing a pet. That is, your Activating Event would be the loss of your pet, due to euthanasia, accident, disappearance, or having had to relinquish it for any other reason.

B stands for your *Belief* about the event. In other words, your *thoughts*. Notice that your thoughts come before your feelings. According to Ellis, your thoughts can be either rational or irrational. Let's use the same irrational thought we used earlier. Imagine that you have run over your cat, leading you to think and believe that you are the world's worst pet guardian. Is this a rational or irrational thought? Is it really possible that you, out of all the pet guardians in the world, are the worst possible guardian? Probably not. However, if you hold on to this thought, repeating it over and over in your mind, you continue to beat yourself up, and you allow yourself to feel bad about yourself for much longer than is necessary. A more rational thought would go like this: "It was a horrible accident, I wish it hadn't happened, and I will be more careful in the future." You will still feel sad, but you will not continue to punish yourself with the "if onlys" and the "shoulds."

C stands for the *Consequences* of your belief. These are your feelings. Again, notice that they come after your thoughts, although most people recognize them sooner. There are four major feelings:

o   Mad

o   Sad

o   Glad

o   Afraid

Everything else is a thought. So, when you say, "I feel so guilty," you're really feeling mad, sad, afraid, or glad (relieved) or maybe even a combination of two or more of those feelings. For example, if your companion animal died accidentally, you might feel mad, sad, and afraid, all at the same time. However, try to remember that all these feelings stem from thoughts, be they rational or irrational. If you can change your thoughts, your feelings will eventually change, too.

D stands for what Ellis calls *Disputing*. By that he means, *Dispute your beliefs*. This concept can be an effective tool to help you move beyond guilty thoughts. For example, imagine that you have lost a pet because of a terminal illness, and you tell yourself that it's all your fault; you should have done this, that, or the other thing to save your friend's life. Dispute that idea. Pretend an attorney is questioning you. The questions would go like this: "Where's the evidence it was your fault? Didn't you do the very best you could? Do you really think you had the power to stop the inevitable?" You'll find that if you dispute your beliefs, they'll begin to lose their power over you.

E stands for *Effective Rational Beliefs (ERB)*. Once you have disputed your beliefs, you can begin to replace them with a more logical and rational belief. Again, using the example of losing a companion animal to a terminal disease, you might say something like, "I had no power over my pet's illness," or "The treatments may not have saved my pet, but I did all I could." When you replace your irrational beliefs with effective rational beliefs, you will be well on your way to overcoming guilt.

Activity: Identify Your Distorted Thinking

First, let's apply the ABC's you just learned. Complete the following chart to take yourself through the process of moving from *Activating Event* to *Effective Rational Beliefs*.

(A) Activating Event: Describe the event that produced your current feelings, i.e., the loss of your companion animal.

(C) Consequence: Describe the consequence of the activating event, i.e., the way you are feeling.

(B) Beliefs: List the irrational beliefs that led to your consequence.

(D) Dispute: Dispute each irrational belief.

(E) Effective Rational Beliefs (ERB): Describe an effective rational belief to counter an irrational belief.

Example: **Belief:** I am the world's worst pet guardian.
Dispute: Am I really the world's worst pet guardian?
ERB: I'm sure there's another pet guardian who's worse than I am.

Belief: I should have known something was wrong with my pet.

Dispute: _____

_____

_____

ERB: _____

_____

_____

Belief: I should have watched my pet every minute.

Dispute: _____

_____

_____

ERB: _____

_____

_____

Belief: I should have gotten a second or a third opinion.

Dispute: _____

_____

_____

ERB: _____

_____

_____

Belief: My cat hated me—that's why she ran away.

Dispute: _____

_____

_____

ERB: _____

_____

_____

Belief: I don't deserve a pet.

Dispute: _____

_____

_____

ERB: _____

_____

_____

Belief: Why me? It isn't fair!

Dispute: _____

_____

_____

ERB: _____

_____

_____

Belief: I should have had more money.

Dispute: _____

_____

_____

ERB: _____

_____

_____

Belief: (*Fill in your own belief.*) _____

Dispute: _____

_____

_____

ERB: _____

_____

Belief: (*Fill in your own belief.*)

Dispute: _____

_____

_____

ERB: _____

_____

_____

Activity: Change Your Distorted Thinking

As listed below, Ellis describes many styles of distorted thinking that create irrational thoughts. Read the fourteen examples of distorted thinking listed below to see if any apply to you. You may identify some that you use more frequently than others. These are the ones that you need to be most aware of, so that an inner alarm sounds whenever they begin to cloud your thinking.

Common forms of distorted thinking include the following:

1. **Filtering:** You take the negative details of a situation and magnify them while filtering out all positive aspects of the situation.

2. **Polarized Thinking:** You see things as either black or white, good or bad. You have to be perfect or you're a failure. You make no allowances for gray areas or middle grounds.

3. **Overgeneralization:** You come to a conclusion based on a single incident or piece of information. If something bad happens, you expect it to happen over and over again.

4. **Mind Reading:** You think you know what others are thinking and feeling and why they act the way they do. You especially think you know how they feel about you.

5. **Catastrophizing:** You expect disaster. You see or hear about a problem and start with the "What ifs." What if tragedy strikes? What if I take my dog to the veterinarian and he or she finds cancer—even though there is no particular reason to believe cancer is likely?

6. **Personalization:** You think that everything that people do or say has something to do with you.

7. **Control Fallacies:** You see yourself as a victim of whatever circumstances are out there. You don't realize that you have control over your own pain and happiness.

8. **Fallacy of Fairness:** You feel resentful because you think that you know what is fair, but others don't always agree with you. You believe things should be fair.

9. **Blaming:** You hold others responsible for your pain, or take the other extreme and believe you are to blame for everything.

10. **Shoulds:** You have a list of rules about how you and other people should act. People who break these rules anger you and you think you are guilty if you violate the rules.

11. **Emotional Reasoning:** You believe that what you *feel* must be true.

12. **Fallacy of Change:** You expect others to change to suit your needs. You need to change people because your hopes for happiness seem to depend entirely on them.

13. **Global Labeling:** You generalize one or two qualities into an entire judgment about a person or event.

14. **Being Right:** You are continually on trial to prove that you are right. Being wrong is unthinkable and you will go to any length to prove you are right, even when it is not in your best interest to do so.

When each distortion in thinking takes place, your job is to change your thoughts, right then and right there. For each of your favorite (or most used) distortions, try to think of examples of what precisely you are thinking when you slip into distorted thinking. Then change to a more rational or logical way of thinking (effective rational belief). Write down the effective rational belief so that you will remember it for future use. The benefit to you will be that your feelings will change, helping you get through the grieving process a little faster and a little easier.

You should now have a pretty good idea of the way you think and what distortion styles you use. If you keep practicing changing the thoughts that do not help you in your life, you will find that not only does the grieving process move a little more easily and quickly but you will also feel better about yourself and less guilty than you did when you began this journey.

So far, we have shown you the basic steps you can take to help yourself through the process of grieving for your pet. In the next chapters, we show you how to apply these basic steps to several difficult situations, including how to care for yourself while caring for a chronically or terminally ill companion animal, and how to manage the painful and exhausting experience of euthanizing a pet. We also will suggest ways to deal with trauma for the guardians of companion animals who witness the violent or brutal deaths of their pets—or who accidentally kill their companion animals.

Chapter 5

Quality of Life at the End of Life

Hope is necessary in every condition.

—Samuel Johnson

Bob and Darcy, a couple in their early forties, listened carefully to what their veterinarian was saying. Their twelve-year-old cat, Clark, had just been diagnosed with diabetes. The veterinarian told them that although they could treat Clark with insulin, there was no cure. Furthermore, the diabetes could lead to future complications, any one of which potentially could be fatal.

The news was devastating to both Bob and Darcy. Clark was one of a litter of kittens born to a mama cat who had been hit by a car and killed shortly after giving birth. A local shelter had had volunteers who took care of the new kittens around the clock, and when they were old enough, Bob and Darcy had adopted two, naming them Clark Kent and Katherine Hepburn.

Bob and Darcy had a special affection for Clark, especially since Katie had died some years earlier, and it didn't take much discussion for them to agree that they wanted to do whatever they could to make his final days comfortable and happy. As long as he wasn't in pain, they were willing to take extraordinary steps to provide for his care. This included giving him twice-daily injections of insulin.

Clark took it all in stride, and even though his condition steadily deteriorated and he eventually lost his eyesight, he seemed to revel in all the extra love and attention that Bob and Darcy lavished on him. When his heart finally gave out one winter morning, the couple took comfort in the fact that they had been with him all the time, tenderly caring for him right up to the moment of his natural death.

What Bob and Darcy provided for Clark was hospice care. They knew there was no hope for his recovery, but they were committed to his care, peace, and comfort until the end. If you have ever cared for a companion animal who is elderly and frail, or is at the end-stage of a terminal illness, you probably already have some understanding of what it means to give hospice care to a beloved pet. Maybe you've had to get up in the middle of the night to help your friend go outside. Maybe you've had to medicate frequently, often at times that weren't convenient for you, or maybe you had to subcutaneously hydrate your pet.

If you have done or are doing any of these things for your pet, it means that you have not given up hope that your companion will make it through, just a little longer, peacefully and comfortably. Nevertheless, no matter how committed you are to providing for your pet in its final days, you might find yourself asking, "Why me? Why my pet?"

Such thoughts and feelings are all normal responses to an extremely difficult situation. As veterinary medicine has advanced, so, too, has the life expectancy of many animals. They are living longer by means of advanced medical interventions, and some pet guardians are rethinking how they want to handle the final days with their beloved pet.

These are the issues that we will cover in this chapter. The goal is to help you find the following:

1. Ways to deal with your companion's health needs

2. Ways to take care of yourself, and

3. Ways to deal with your feelings, so there is a peaceful quality of life for both of you at the end of your pet's life.

The Hope of Hospice

You probably are at least somewhat familiar with the concept of hospice, but you might be surprised to learn, much to the pleasure of animal lovers everywhere, that hospice care is now being formally developed for companion animals. As the great songwriter Bob Dylan said, "The times, they are a-changin." And, in the eyes of many pet guardians, the change that offers hospice care for companion animals couldn't be more welcome. For many years veterinary medicine has been developing a hospice program similar to what we now have for human beings. In April 2001, the American Veterinary Medical Association approved the *Guidelines for Veterinary Hospice Care*. At this time, widespread hospice care for pets is more a vision than a reality, but it is clear that the veterinary profession now recognizes animals as more than "just pets."

What is hospice and what does it do? For a better understanding, you might find it interesting to learn about the history of the hospice movement for human beings. The word "hospice" comes from the Latin *hospes*, meaning a way-station. In medieval times, a *hospes* was a sort of hostel where travelers could rest and refresh themselves before continuing their journey.

In the 1960s, a number of people saw the need to give just such comfort to terminally ill people, who, even with aggressive medical treatment, had no chance of recovering. Pioneer hospice workers suggested that, rather than continuing to apply heroic measures to keep the dying alive, it was more appropriate to relieve them of their pain and assure them of the right to die with dignity.

What Is Hospice Care for Humans?

In 1947, at St. Thomas' Hospital in London, Dame Cicely Saunders, an English physician, met David Tasma, a young Jewish refugee who was alone and dying of cancer. The experience was a watershed for Dame Saunders. Their conversations and her care for him inspired her to seek ways to provide a larger support system for the terminally ill.

She began by looking at the needs of the terminally ill, and her research revealed a lack of coherent social and medical support for those whose conditions were fatal (Saunders 1990). Dame Saunders realized that there was a need not only for more homes for the dying but also for an entirely new approach to meeting their medical, psychological, and spiritual needs, while at the same time giving support to family members. By the early 1960s, Saunders had assembled a group to help establish a new kind of home for the dying of London that would also serve as a research and education center. News of her ideas quickly spread, and in 1967 her efforts resulted in the opening of St. Christopher's Hospice in London, England.

The first hospice in the United States was built in New Haven, Connecticut, in 1971 and is similar to the design of St. Christopher's. Today there are more than 3,500 hospices in the United States. However, at this time, there are very few hospicelike facilities for companion animals. I believe that, as veterinary medicine advances, there will come a time when hospice care for pets will be as viable a resource for pet guardians as it is for human beings.

What Is Hospice Care for Pets?

Hospice care is compassionate care administered to your companion animal prior to euthanasia or natural death. It focuses on the quality and comfort of a pet's final days rather than on the specific treatment of any disease. Hospice is a philosophy, not a physical place. Its main concern is living and dying with dignity. Hospice provides kind, safe, pain-free, end-of-life care at home for the animal companion.

Unlike the human hospice, in which the physician gives the patient one year or less to live, veterinary hospice does not estimate the life expectancy of the animal. However, it is understood by you and your veterinarian that there is no treatment that will cure your pet's disease. As a result, you will be administering to chronically and/or terminally ill pets.

These are some typical chronic diseases that might necessitate hospice care for your pet:

o   Chronic kidney disease

o   Chronic liver disease

o   Chronic pancreatitis

o   Heart disease

o   Arthritis

o   Chronic skin disease

o   Chronic ear disease

o   Diabetes mellitus

o   Irritable bowel syndrome

Situations that might be considered terminal and could call for hospice care would include the following:

o   Cancer that has spread outside the area in which it started

o   Cancer that is in both the chest and the abdominal cavity

o   Liver, kidney, and heart disease that have progressed into failure

Applying the principles of hospice care to terminally ill animals seems a natural choice. The pet's human companions benefit from the opportunity to do special things for their pet, such as providing special treats and the gift of their time and energy. Hospice care gives the family and you time to say good-bye. The pet benefits during hospice care from the many contributions to its quality of life—extra physical affection, favorite food treats, and extra one-on-one time with family members. However, choosing hospice care is not an easy decision. There are many factors to weigh if you are considering hospice-type care for your pet.

Activity: Exploring the Hospice Option

Before moving on, this might be the time to consider whether your companion animal fits the criteria for hospice care. Are you ready to put a stop to any heroic measures and accept that your companion will be receiving palliative care instead of medical treatment? In other words, your pet will receive care that will make it more comfortable but will not attempt to cure the disease. If you are not comfortable with that type of care, then hospice is not for you. Talk to your veterinarian about all the treatments available to your pet before you decide.

Hospice Care for Your Pets

Hospice care cannot be provided without the help of a caring, understanding veterinarian. To understand what to expect, you need to know what to look for, so that when new symptoms appear, you won't panic. Remember, animals can sense your anxiety, so you need to learn to relax. You will need a veterinarian who will prescribe medications for pain, and teach you how to administer subcutaneous fluids, give injections, and whatever else it might take. You have to be sure you can do what needs to be done.

For example, what will you do if you have a 95-pound dog who needs to be carried outside to urinate, and you weigh only 120 pounds? As much as you may want to do this for your dog, it may be an impossible task. Unless you can find someone to help you carry the dog, you may have no option other than to let your pet go painlessly.

If you do choose hospice care, you need a diagnostic and treatment plan from your veterinarian.

Questions to Ask Your Veterinarian

o   What are your estimates of my pet's survival time, with and without hospice care?

o   What kind of drugs will we use, and how will they affect my pet?

o   What are the benefits and/or side effects of the drugs we will use?

o   Will my pet be comfortable, even if the disease can't be cured?

o   How often will I have to bring my pet in to see you?

o   How do I go about getting the appropriate medication?

o   What options are available for hospice care for my pet in my city and/or elsewhere?

o   How many times a day will I have to pill, hydrate, or inject my pet?

o   Can I miss a day?

o   Will you or your assistant come to my home if necessary?

o   What will be the approximate cost of the treatment over the long run?

Activity: What Do You Consider Essential for Hospice Care?

Make a list of the criteria for hospice care that you consider essential for a good quality of life for your pet. Before you make your list, discuss the criteria with your family, as opinions may vary. For example, will it be enough that Fido is alive, even though he can't chase his ball the way he once did? Or does your child want Fido restored to health to be exactly as he once was? If it's not enough just to keep Fido alive, hospice may not be the answer for you and your family.

Questions to Ask Yourself

It's important to be honest with yourself when you are considering hospice care for your friend. You know yourself better than anyone else does, and you know your pet. Before you make a decision, ask yourself the following questions, and answer them as honestly as you can.

Can I psychologically handle seeing my pet continually get worse? Watching a pet deteriorate may be more than some can handle, especially because there is no way to explain to the pet exactly what's going on. Even though your companion animal probably will not suffer during hospice care, its quality of life will surely diminish. Can you handle that prospect?

Can I psychologically handle the change in my relationship with my pet? Your companion may begin to resent being medicated, poked, and prodded, and it may start to run away from you. Additionally, your companion may need to be carried outside, to its litter box, or up and down stairs. You might need to interrupt your schedule or come home from work to do these things. If there is someone else in your family who is not as bonded to your pet as you are, sometimes it's best to let that person do the actual caretaking.

Do I feel it's cruel to keep my pet alive? What are my spiritual beliefs regarding euthanasia? These two questions go hand in hand. If you are a strong supporter of euthanasia for companion animals, you might feel that prolonging your friend's life would be cruel. On the other hand, if you feel that you don't have the right to take your pet's life, hospice may be a better choice for you.

Can I afford the time and money hospice care will take? Although this may seem like a mercenary subject, you must consider the time and monetary demands that hospice care will place on you and your family. Consider your own tolerance level for nursing care. Don't beat yourself up if you can't do it. Hospice care takes a lot of time, money, and effort. Not everyone has the ability to provide all of these at the same time.

Unlike human hospice, you, a friend, or a family member will have to be the major caretaker, as animal hospice care has not yet evolved in veterinary medicine the way that it has in human medicine. Therefore, it will be hard or impossible to find nurses to come in and administer medications, give the pet baths, or even give you a break. Can you handle this?

Does my family feel the same as I do about hospice care? If you live within a family system, that system will be disrupted. You may be willing to accept the demands of hospice care, but you must also acknowledge the demands it will place on the other members of your family. Even if you are the family member doing the major part of the caretaking, this will result in time taken away from your family and their usual routines. Is everyone ready to accept these sacrifices?

Do I want to remember the last days with my pet this way? Imagery is very powerful. It's entirely possible that your lasting memories of your pet will be of the final, declining days, when your friend was completely dependent on you for its every need. Even if you are able to retain happy memories of better times with your beloved companion, the images from the end-of-life days will stay with you, too. Do you think you can synthesize such different kinds of memories?

How do you think your pet might feel about hospice care? This may seem like a foolish question, because how can we ever know how our companion animals really think or feel? But we *do* know our pets; we know their habits, their likes and dislikes, and their idiosyncrasies. My friend Louise was considering hospice care for her cat, Alex, when he was diagnosed with feline infectious peritonitis. Her veterinarian had assured her that they could keep Alex comfortable until the end with medication and a drainage procedure. But Louise asked herself this question, and she knew that Alex would have hated it. He had always hated visits to the veterinarian, and having to endure pills and shots was even worse. He cried pitifully when they were forced on him. That decided it for her. She knew Alex would not have appreciated hospice care, and that was the crucial factor in her decision.

Practical Tips for Hospice Care

If you choose hospice care, here are a few practical tips that might make you and your pet a little more comfortable. Ask your veterinarian for other ideas that might fit the exact needs of your companion animal.

o   If your pet is incontinent, use diapers as a way to limit the amount of urine or feces that actually gets into your house.

o   Your pet should be kept clean and comfortable. If urine gets on the animal's skin, it can scald it, and your pet can get an infection from it.

o   Rotate your pet so he or she won't get bed sores. It's nice to have a soft, padded bed for your pet to lie on.

o   Don't ignore lumps of any kind. Get them checked out as soon as you notice them.

o   If your pet is arthritic and cannot climb stairs, you might have to change the environment. For example, your dog or cat may have to be kept either upstairs or downstairs all the time, and you might have to erect a barrier at the head or the foot of the stairs. Adapt the environment to make your pet comfortable.

o   If your cat has a hard time getting into the litter box you have now, get a low-edge litter box.

o   If you get angry and frustrated, remember, it's not your fault, it's not the veterinarian's fault, and it's certainly not the animal's fault that this is happening.

o   Ask for help if you need it.

Taking Care of Yourself

Since the job of taking care of your companion animal will be difficult if you choose hospice care, you must remember that taking care of yourself is just as critical. If you don't take good care of yourself, you will not be able to help your pet. Here are some suggestions for self-care through this both difficult and rewarding time.

Find or create a support network. Your network can be made up of family, friends, other caregivers, your veterinarian or veterinary staff members, whatever works for you. Make sure these people understand why you are doing hospice care for your companion. If they don't understand, they should not be a part of your support team. If you have trouble finding a support team, get on the Internet and go to one of the many Web sites that are listed in the Resources section in the back of this book. You will find chat rooms and bulletin boards where you can communicate with others who have experience with what you are going through.

Don't be afraid to ask for help. It's hard, sometimes impossible, to manage hospice care by yourself. There are others who will help. If you can't enlist the help of a friend or family member, ask your veterinarian for a referral to someone who might be willing to lend you a hand.

Give yourself some time off. Even if it's just a walk to a park or anywhere else that you find peaceful and relaxing, it's important for you to take a break now and then. Find a pet sitter who is qualified to care for your pet in your absence, if needed.

Practice deep breathing or meditation. I have found that if I am having a very stressful or frustrating day, it helps to stop, sit quietly for a few minutes, clear my mind, and take several deep, slow, and calming breaths. Inhale from the abdomen deeply on a slow count of four. Hold that breath for a second or two, then exhale slowly on a count of four. Continue this until you feel a little calmer and more relaxed.

Forgive yourself for whatever you think you have done wrong. No one can do it all, and you are doing the best that you can. That is all any of us can do. If you are thinking that you are guilty of something, reread chapter 4.

Exercise to relieve anger, stress, or frustration. This is a hard job, and you need to be physically as well as emotionally healthy to be as effective as you can.

Get enough rest and focus on good nutrition. Obviously you need to maintain your own good health in order to be able to provide quality care for your pet. Be watchful, however, and avoid overeating or sleeping more than necessary as a way to avoid the emotional pain that hospice care sometimes entails.

Seek the help of a mental health professional, if necessary. If caring for your pet gets to be emotionally too much for you, don't hesitate to use the services of a mental health professional. Sometimes just talking helps.

Hospice care for companion animals is not for everyone nor for every animal. Weigh your decision carefully, making sure that you, your family, and your veterinarian are all on the same team. It will be hard work, full of good days and bad days. There are no right or wrong decisions, as each case is unique, with its own set of circumstances. No matter what you choose, remember, you are doing what you think is best for both you and your pet, and isn't that what pet guardianship is really all about?

When hospice care is not an option, or no longer an option, the time may come when euthanasia might be considered as a way to help your com

panion animal pass from this life with dignity and grace. Chapter 6 explores this difficult subject, providing you with the necessary information to help you make the best decision for yourself and your pet.

Chapter 6

Making the Final Choice

Grieve not,
Nor speak of me with tears
But laugh and talk of me
As if I were beside you . . .
I loved you so—
'Twas heaven here with you.

— Isla Paschal Richardson

Christine sat silently as she stroked her precious black Rex rabbit, Velvet. Today was the day she had never wanted to arrive. The House Rabbit Society had told her, when she adopted Velvet as a bunny, that rabbits don't usually live as long as dogs, cats, birds, or reptiles. She had wanted the cuddly creature anyway, and like most of us, she didn't think ahead to the day when she might have to make a decision to end her companion's life.

Now, eight years later, Velvet needed Christine to make the toughest decision she possibly could. The very word "euthanasia" made her cry. How could she do this to her friend? Was it really the right time? Should she get another veterinarian's opinion? Did she have the right to play God? Her inner voice was asking so many questions, and yet she knew it had to be done. Velvet was in too much pain from the cancer to let her go on any longer. Euthanasia could be the last humane thing she could do for her friend.

She got up, put Velvet in her comfortable cage, and took her to the veterinary hospital. After asking the doctor once more if there was anything else they could do for her precious rabbit, and receiving the same answer, she agreed to painlessly end Velvet's life. She held her while the veterinarian and his assistant calmly and compassionately inserted the injection that would stop Velvet's heart. Velvet died quietly and peacefully, all the while looking at Christine. There was love in her eyes, as if to say "thank you."

The Historical Background of Euthanasia

The term "euthanasia" is derived from the Greek word meaning "happy or fortunate in death." It has been most commonly associated with a merciful or peaceful termination of life to avoid torment or pain from a fatal or incurable disease. Although not much has been written about the origins of euthanasia for companion animals, we can get some idea of how long the practice has been going on by looking at the literature on euthanasia for human beings.

The practice of euthanasia has been accepted in some form by various cultures, groups, or societies throughout recorded history. Among the wise men of ancient Greece, ending one's life for a variety of reasons, pain and illness included, was considered a rational and humane thing to do (Westendorf 1996). In ancient Greece and Rome, helping others to die was considered permissible in some situations. Voluntary euthanasia for the elderly was an approved custom in several ancient societies, as long as the person and his or her family agreed. In some Eskimo cultures, an old or sick Eskimo would tell the family that he or she was ready to die, and the family, if it was a good one, would immediately comply by abandoning the aged person to the ravages of nature or by killing the old or sick person.

The first organizations to promote legalization of voluntary euthanasia in the United States were formed in the 1930s. In the late 1970s, the pro-euthanasia movement gained significant momentum after a highly publicized tragedy in 1975. A twenty-one-year-old woman named Karen Ann Quinlan suffered respiratory arrest that resulted in severe and irreversible brain damage, leaving her in a coma. Several months later, after the doctors informed her parents that it was unlikely that she would ever recover, Karen's parents requested that the artificial means of life support be removed. The hospital refused. After a lengthy battle, the New Jersey Supreme Court ruled that the Quinlans could disconnect the device so that Karen could "die with dignity."

Perhaps knowing some of the historical perspectives on euthanasia can help us to appreciate how much we care for our companion animals when we allow them the right to die with dignity. There are many human beings who would like that right to be extended to them. Some might say that we have more compassion for our pets than we do for ourselves. Whether this is true or not has been a source of considerable discussion for philosophers, scholars, clergy, psychologists, and the medical profession, and it's likely that the debate will continue for many years to come.

However, we do have the right to make this choice for our companion animals. Some argue it is the last humane thing we can do for our friends. Even so, it is never an easy decision. Let us look at some of the ways you might be able to recognize when the time to say good-bye has come. Before reading further, however, you might want to consider doing the following activity.

Activity: List Arguments for and Against Euthanasia

Make a list of arguments for and against euthanasia for companion animals as if you were a part of a discussion group. Consider it from the perspective of your particular situation. The hope is that by doing this activity you will achieve some clarity to help you with making your own decision.

Questions and Answers

Making the decision to euthanize is often harder than dealing with the loss itself. Many people say that they can accept death and the accompanying grief, but they have great difficulty being the one to decide to end their companion's life.

As you face this painful decision, perhaps the following questions will serve as a guide. If you don't have the information that you need to guide you, consult your veterinarian. He or she will be there to provide answers to some of these difficult questions.

- o   Is there a reasonable chance for a cure? For comfort?

- o   How much additional time might treatment give my companion? What will the quality of that time be like?

- o   Do I have the financial and emotional resources to handle long-term medical care, if it is required?

- o   Will I have the necessary physical and emotional stamina to attend to my pet's needs?

- o   How many of my pet's usual activities are still possible?

- o   Is my pet suffering, even though physical pain is not evident?

- o   What do I think my pet would want?

- o   If I were in my pet's place, what would I want?

- o   Is my pet in pain?

- o   Are there severe behavioral problems (such as aggression that hasn't been tempered by training or medication) that compromise the safety and well-being of my pet or others?

- o   How do I feel about euthanasia? Will I be okay with my decision?

- o   Considering the temperament of my particular companion animal, how will it respond psychologically to the treatment, if treatment is available?

Let your answers to these questions guide you in your decision-making process. Remember, there probably will never be an exact "right" time. You can do only your best with the information that you have gathered.

Some people say that your pet will tell you when it's time. Although this may be true in some cases, most pets are the descendants of animals with long histories of living wild before they were domesticated. As a result, most pets are somewhat hardwired not to show it when they are in pain or distressed. This built-in, self-protective mechanism originally functioned as a defense from their predators. What this means for you is that you can't always count on your companion to be the one to let you know when the time has come. You are the guardian, and just as if your pet were a child that could not speak, it is important that you make a decision that is right for both of you.

When I decided to euthanize my beloved cat, Jasmine, I asked myself all of the questions above. Some of them did not apply, others did. In my final assessment, I believed that, even if I continued treatment for Jasmine, she would have had to be medicated and hydrated each day. I didn't feel it was fair to her, as she was not the kind of cat that took easily to being pilled and hydrated. I tried treatment for a while, but she soon began to run from me, hiding under the bed when I approached her. She began to distrust me and kept her distance, even when it wasn't pill time.

In the end, I could only believe that she would be happier not having to go through what must have been traumatic for her. It was at this time I decided it was time to let her go. Although there were still treatments available, I knew she was never going to get much better, and I let her die with dignity. Personally, I have never regretted this decision, although she will always have a special place in my heart.

A Humane Ending for a Beloved Life

If you're like most people, you don't spend much time thinking about your pet's death while it is still alive and healthy. In fact, people don't usually think about their own deaths and how they would like to die. In his book, *Flashbacks: An Autobiography* (1983), Timothy Leary spoke of his own impending death and he described some of the things that he was doing toward the end of his life. He set up a bed outside so that on nice days he could be in the sunshine and see nature. It was a place where he could be with himself or with friends, and he found it comforting.

In *Tuesdays with Morrie* (1997), Mitch Albom describes his last months with the dying Morrie Schwartz. Morrie teaches a lot of lessons about life, but to him, the most important lesson is to love. Isn't that what we do for our companion animals at the end of their lives? Isn't that what euthanasia is really all about?

If you have made the decision to end your pet's life mercifully, you have some of the same opportunities as humans do when we know we are going to die. What I mean by this is that you can do something special for your pet before you help it die. If, for example, your dog liked a special park, you might want to take him there, even if he can't run and play the way he used to. Maybe your cat liked to sit on your lap outside on the patio with the sun shining. Do this for her. Perhaps there was a favorite toy that your particular companion enjoyed. Take that with your pet to the veterinarian when the day has come, or have it beside your friend if you choose to euthanize at home. These things will not only help your pet, they will also help you to remember that you did something special for your companion at the end.

Activity: Provide Some Pleasure, and Remember Your Pet

1. Think of some things that your pet enjoyed while healthy, and, if possible, do at least one of those things for your companion before you help him or her on the final journey.

2. Make a list of all of the things that your companion animal taught you. Then list all of the things you taught your pet. Keep that list and use it when and if you decide to hold a memorial for your pet. We will talk more about memorials later in this chapter.

At the End

If you have decided that the end has come for your pet, it might help you to know exactly what to expect. Some people choose to be with their pets at the time of death; others don't. There is no right or wrong decision. It is a personal choice, and only you can make it. When I began running pet-loss support groups, most veterinarians did not allow the guardians to be with their pets at the end, believing that it would be too hard for the person to bear.

Times have changed, and today most veterinarians will give you the option to be with your companion at the end of its life. Try to be guided by what makes you feel comfortable, and by what you think you can live with later. Some people consider being present as a final demonstration of their love to the pet, and they take comfort in knowing that their pet is actually dead and at peace. Others prefer to remember their pet as it was, alive and active. If you choose to be with your companion, ask your veterinarian to explain the procedure so there will be no surprises.

There are also veterinarians who will come to your home to euthanize your pet. This may be something you might want to explore. If you choose to do this, remember that you might come to think of a particular part of your home as the place where your pet was euthanized. This may or may not be something you are psychologically prepared to handle. Think it through, or perhaps you can talk to some others who had their pets euthanized at home. You can also choose to euthanize your companion outdoors at your home, rather than indoors. It might make for a more peaceful setting, especially if you have a yard or an area in a garden that is acceptable to you for this kind of procedure.

The Euthanasia Procedure

Most veterinarians will explain the euthanasia procedure, especially if you ask. However, in case this does not happen or you are unable to ask, here is an explanation of the most commonly used procedure:

The veterinarian or assistant will shave the fur from a leg or another area for a catheter to be taped in place. The pet may squirm or resist; however, it is not because it thinks it's going to die. Animals do not have the same concept of death as humans. It may struggle because it doesn't like being there. Your pet may also be sensing human tension, which may create more anxiety. This part of the process may be done in your presence or in the back of the hospital, so that it is less stressful to all.

A sedative is often infused, giving your pet the opportunity to relax into a tranquil state. At this point, if you have chosen to be with your companion, the veterinarian will bring your pet back into the examination room for you to be close to it when he or she administers the final infusion of a drug (usually pentobarbital) to painlessly stop the heart.

After the infusion of pentobarbital is given, your pet's heart will stop in a few seconds. The body may still twitch or wiggle, or even gasp, but you can be assured that your companion is not in pain. These are normal responses, also seen in human beings. Voiding of the pet's bowel or bladder may also occur, as all of the muscles have relaxed. You may want to close your pet's eyes by pressing its eyelids gently down. Right about now you may be thinking, "I can't do that," but you may be surprised at how much you may want to do this for your pet. However, as stated earlier in this chapter, there is no right or wrong decision about being with your companion at the end. It is a personal choice and no one should make it for you.

You may want some private time with your beloved pet after the event is over. Most veterinarians and their staff are very sensitive to this and will allow you all the time you need. No matter how much you know you've made the right decision, you probably will still feel somewhat psychologically and physically drained after it's over. In fact, you might want to bring someone along with you to comfort you and drive you home.

You may also feel some relief that your pet is no longer suffering. People have told me that when they they feel relief, they often feel guilty. Remember, though, that guilt is a thought, and you can change it. (You may want to review chapter 4.) You have done what you considered to be in the best interest of your beloved companion animal, and you have let go of your desire to keep your pet with you at any cost, to help your beloved die with dignity.

Activity: Ask Questions, Then Decide

1. If you have more questions about what to expect, or about the euthanasia process, ask your veterinarian. He or she will have the answers and will guide you through the procedure. Note that not all veterinarians offer this information in advance, because they may assume you don't want to know. If you do want to know, ask!

2. Decide in advance whether you want to be with your pet when the procedure is being done. Make a list of your thoughts, both for and against being with your pet at the end. Make a decision and write it on the same piece of paper. Keep the list with you when the time has come. If doubts arise and you become unsure, refer to your list and to your final decision.

Taking Care of the Body

If at all possible, it is better to decide what to do with your beloved pet's body before the euthanasia procedure is performed. You may also want to sign the necessary forms and pay for the service in advance, to eliminate the possibility of experiencing any more psychological pain right after the procedure is performed.

If you are considering having an autopsy performed to answer any questions you may have regarding your pet's illness or injury, let your veterinarian know in advance.

There are several answers to the question, "What do I do with my pet's body?" Your veterinarian or an assigned staff member will know what is available. Note that some of the following choices may be unavailable in your particular part of the country.

Cremation

There are two ways an animal's body can be cremated. The first is *individually*, the second *communally*. Individual cremation means that your pet and your pet alone will be cremated. You will get back the ashes (called cremains) of your pet either in a box or an urn (if you have chosen one in advance). Most pet cemeteries provide this service and many of them will pick up your pet's body from the veterinarian's office if you would prefer not to take the body to the cemetery yourself.

Communal cremation is an option for pet guardians who do not need or want to have their pets cremated individually or have the ashes returned to them. In communal cremation, several pets are cremated together and pet cemeteries typically scatter the ashes, either on their grounds, or in natural settings.

Burial

Some people choose to bury their pets in either a pet cemetery or at home. If you choose to bury your pet at home, you should make yourself aware of the laws regarding this type of burial, as it is illegal in some parts of the country. Many people choose a pet cemetery to bury their beloved animals. Check to see if there are any in your area, and go there yourself to see how it feels to you.

Rendering

Many people decide to let the veterinarian deal with their pet's body because it is too difficult or perhaps impossible (as in the case of a large animal) for the guardian to handle. In this case, the veterinarian will have a rendering company pick up your pet's body. It is taken to a business or industrial site where the bodies are used to make animal foods, fertilizer, and other products. This is a way of reusing or recycling your pet's body after its death. Some people like this idea. Their view of this practice is that their pet is still being helpful. No matter what you decide, remember that your pet is no longer living and its spirit or soul has left the body and will always be with you.

Activity: Obtain Information

Gather information about all the ways of dealing with your pet's body. Make your decision before you euthanize, if possible. If you want a pet cemetery to pick up your pet, make plans in advance. If you want to take your pet to the cemetery after the procedure, call once you know when you are going to euthanize. That way, they can be ready for you.

Memorializing Your Companion Animal

Since the eighteenth century, English aristocrats have commemorated the death of their favorite pets with monumental sculptures and florid epitaphs. In the United States, we also have had a love affair with our companion animals' memorials. When your pet dies, you can choose what to do with the body, and how you memorialize your friend. In Gardena, California, a four-and-a-half acre pet cemetery contains the remains of more than 28,000 animals, including the favorite dogs of Edward G. Robinson and Nat "King" Cole. In the United States alone, more than 500 pet cemeteries serve the needs of bereaved pet guardians, and this number is steadily rising.

The concept of animal burial is hardly new. Because of their deep respect for cats, the ancient Egyptians often buried or mummified these revered beings. Their bodies were sometimes wrapped in linen and placed in containers of pottery, wood, stone, or metal. The early Chinese emperors established cemeteries for dogs in Beijing. Queen Victoria erected a cemetery on the Isle of Wight for her pets. The animals of royalty, including Frederick the Great and Catherine of Russia, were interred with honor in cemeteries founded exclusively for them, or in private family plots. In the United States, archeological excavations have revealed that various native tribes buried companion animals with respect and ceremony (Beauchamp 2000).

So, what might *you* do to memorialize your companion animal? It doesn't matter whether you have the body or the cremains; even without them, you can still create a special event to commemorate your pet's life. If you think about it, memorial services are not held for those who died, but for the living. Memorials are a way of showing how much we cared for the life we have lost, as well as a way to begin to put closure on the first step of the grieving process, which is denial.

Over the many years that I have been doing pet-loss counseling, many people have told me about the rituals and ceremonies that they performed to memorialize their companion animals. The following list describes some of those ceremonies. Perhaps some will appeal to you.

o Hold some kind of memorial service for your pet. Include anyone, children, too, who might have loved your companion animal. At the service, read a poem or a story, or say a prayer that fits the occasion. You don't need a body to do this. You can use a picture of your pet. Position the picture somewhere appropriate and hold the memorial service in front of the picture.

o Light a candle in memory of your beloved friend each Monday evening. In fact, for many pet guardians, this has become a new tradition. Information about this ceremony can be found online at <http://petloss.com>.

o Write or tape record special memories and anecdotes of your friend. Have friends and family add to your list, so that all can share their memories.

o Make something that reminds you of your pet, such as a drawing, a clay sculpture, needlework, a paw print, or any other creative idea you might have.

o Keep some fur, teeth, mane hairs, or something else from your pet. Place these mementos in a special place, such as a beautiful box or locket.

o Make a donation in memory of your pet to a cause or organization that you think your pet might like.

o If you have your pet's ashes, you might want to place them in an urn and put it somewhere in your home. Or you might choose to scatter the ashes in a place that was special to your pet. You can even do both: keep some of the ashes and scatter the rest.

o Keep your pet's tags. You can place these on a key ring so that you can carry the memory of your special friend with you.

o If you bury your pet, have a headstone made with your pet's name on it, as well as anything else you might want to add. You might even wrap one of your pet's toys around the headstone.

o Plant a tree or a bush in honor of your pet.

o   If you like to write, consider writing a story or an article for your local newspaper about how the loss of your pet has affected you. There are others who would appreciate knowing that they are not alone in their grief.

o   Attend a pet-loss support group.

Helping Children to Cope with Euthanasia

The choice to euthanize a beloved companion animal is difficult enough for adults faced with making this decision. Helping your children, or other children, understand and accept that the time has come to help the pet die may be equally or even more difficult

In trying to protect a child from grief, parents sometimes make the mistake of minimizing, or completely avoiding, the pain caused by the death of the family pet. By doing this, parents may miss an important opportunity to teach their children a powerful lesson about coping with the painful reality of death.

The relationships between children and pets are often different from adult relationships with their pets. Children's pets are often considered their best friends, their confidants, their playmates. When that bond is broken, the pain the child feels can be very intense and can result in feelings of insecurity, anxiety, anger, guilt, helplessness, distrust, and fear. The relationships that children have with their pets are often so special that an entire chapter of this book is devoted to the subject. (See chapter 8.) However, right now, let's look at some of the ways you can help your child deal with euthanasia:

o   Be as open and as honest as you can be. If you know your pet is terminally ill, tell your children as soon as possible, so that they won't hear it from someone else. If they find out that you have distorted the truth or lied to them, they might learn not to trust you in the future.

o   Avoid using euphemisms like "put to sleep." These terms can confuse a child because going to sleep implies waking up again. Of course, this is not the case with euthanasia.

o   Offer age-appropriate explanations, and be available to answer questions. (More on age-appropriate explanations can be found in chapter 8.) Children do need to know that grief is normal and that it is okay to cry and to feel sad. You might explain that the adults, too, feel sad and that this is how we all feel when we lose someone we love.

o   Make sure that the child understands that it is the pet's death that is making you sad, and not something that the child did. Children often think that a parent's sadness is somehow their fault. Reassure them that there wasn't anything they could do to help the pet, and that its demise is not their fault. Help young children understand why euthanasia is sometimes necessary. One good way to explain this to them might be to tell them that their pet's body stopped working and just won't work anymore. Explain that their pet may have been suffering from old age ("When an animal gets old, his body wears out and stops working; animals do not live as long as we do, so they usually die before us.") Their pet may have had a terminal illness ("Fluffy had a disease that couldn't be fixed, or treated with medicine"). Or, their pet may have been in an accident ("A terrible thing happened to Spot, he got hit by a car, and his body was so badly hurt that it couldn't be fixed").

o   Include children in the decision to use euthanasia, if they are old enough to understand. This will give them the opportunity to say good-bye, and to make the most of whatever time they have left with their pet.

o   Decide if you want your child or children to be present when the procedure is performed. If they want to be present, explain what will happen in a way that they will understand. Remember, you are helping your pet to die with dignity, and euthanasia means "peaceful death." It is often best to allow children to be present during the procedure, *if they want to be there.* Sometimes, the reality of a peaceful death is far less traumatic to children than their terrible fantasies about it. If your child does not want to be present during the procedure, give him or her the opportunity to see their pet after it has died. This will reinforce the reality and remove some of the mystery and fear of death. Don't force your children to participate, however, as they may not be psychologically ready for this kind of experience.

o   Hold a memorial service for your pet. The whole family can participate in this event.

Over the years, many people have asked me whether they should get a new pet right away. Although I never give a definite answer, as this must be an individual, personal decision, I do not encourage it. Getting another pet too soon may imply to children that their grief is unimportant and unnecessary since everything is replaceable anyway. Also, they may react with anger or guilt, and reject the new pet because to accept it would be felt as disloyalty to the pet who died. When most of your family members feel ready to adopt a new pet, the children should be included in the selection process and be actively involved.

It is my hope that this information will help you to help your children in dealing with one of the hardest decisions anyone who loves a companion animal will ever have to make. Remember that your child loved your pet, too, and will also grieve when your pet is gone. Mourning the lost pet can bring the whole family closer and become a time to reflect on how much you love each other.

Activities: For Children to Remember Their Pets

o   Draw or write about your pet. Include a description of his or her personality. Was your pet shy, happy, playful, cuddly, a good listener, and so forth?

o   What do you miss about your pet? Is there something that you miss the most? Write it down, so that you can remember.

o   Talk to adults about your feelings.

o   Make a list of some of the things that comfort you, such as talking, hugging, eating certain foods, playing certain games, reading, playing music, drawing, punching a pillow, crying. Try to do some of these things, so that you won't feel quite so bad.

o   Who can you talk to about how you feel? Talk to that person if you can. Maybe you have more than one person you can talk to. It's okay to talk and it's okay to cry, to be angry, and to feel very sad.

By now, you should have the information you need to make and carry out the decision to euthanize your companion animal. For me, it is truly the last humane thing I can do for a beloved pet. If, however, after reading this chapter, you decide that euthanasia is not an option for you and your pet, you will have arrived at that decision in a reasoned and informed manner.

In the next chapter, we will look at how we can deal with the death of a companion animal in which we either played a part in contributing to that death, or had to watch die in a violent manner that we could not prevent. We will also look at dealing with the death of a companion animal who was not only your beloved pet but also a service animal that allowed you to lead a more independent life.

Chapter 7

Horrible Images, Terrible Thoughts

You gain inner strength, courage, and confidence by every experience in which you really stop to look fear in the face. You are able to say to yourself, "I lived through this horror. I can take the next thing that comes along."

—Eleanor Roosevelt

Dealing with Trauma and Post-Traumatic Stress Syndrome

Before you start: This chapter is for those of you who have actually witnessed (or perhaps imagined) the violent or traumatic death of your pet. It is also for those who have (or have had), a service animal who died or had to be relinquished. If none of this has been your experience, you may want to skip this chapter and move on to the next, chapter 8. The stories here are all true, but they may be too vivid and disturbing for you to read. However, if you have had the unfortunate experience of seeing or experiencing this kind of death of your beloved friend, you may find that reading this chapter will be helpful. In this chapter we provide you with some tools to deal with the horrible images and terrible thoughts that you may be experiencing. It is also important to point out that, although the general intent of this book is to help you help yourself, the kind of trauma that you might experience from witnessing a violent loss may not lend itself to self-help measures. Therefore, we also suggest that after reading this chapter, you may want to consult a mental health professional. We offer guidelines for the kinds of questions to ask a mental health professional, along with descriptions of the different types of therapy that are often effective for post-traumatic stress disorder.

Carolyn's Story

It was a beautiful, chamber-of-commerce day in San Diego. Carolyn's three dogs, Toby, Andrea, and Dynamite, led her to the front door in anticipation of their morning walk. Toby, her large black standard poodle, already had his leash in his mouth. Andrea and Dynamite were eager, too, and soon all three had been leashed and were ready to go. It was a ritual they had shared since all the dogs had been puppies. Toby was going on eight years old, but never tired of the walks. Andrea, a smaller version of her big brother, was five, and Dynamite, who weighed in at four pounds, was almost four years old. No one was ever sure exactly what breed Dynamite was, but all agreed she looked a little like a small seal in a dog's body. She was called Dyna for short. The dogs were devoted to Carolyn, who had rescued them all from the animal shelter when they were pups.

Carolyn, too, enjoyed these morning walks. There was a trail leading through her housing development, and she never tired of watching her dogs sniff at a bush or try to chase an imaginary creature. Carolyn taught fifth grade in an impoverished area, and her working days were often long and difficult. These morning walks helped her to clear her thoughts to begin her day.

On this particular Wednesday, they were about halfway through their walk when Carolyn noticed a large dog, what looked like a Doberman mix, running rapidly toward them. It was not on a leash, and she could see no person supervising the animal. Before she could do anything to protect herself or her pets, the Doberman had his large jaws around Dynamite's head. Dyna screamed and Carolyn's other dogs wrenched and pulled on their leashes. Carolyn was unable to hold on to her dogs, and as she fell to the ground, the Doberman picked Dyna up by the throat and shook her as if she were a stuffed animal. There was blood everywhere. The other dogs ran, not knowing what to do. Carolyn screamed for help, and finally the guardian of the Doberman came out of her house to see what was going on.

She had "let her dog out for some air," as she put it, and she insisted her dog had never attacked another animal before. Since she had a small baby, she continued, she couldn't walk the dog and take care of the baby, too. Carolyn asked her to at least take her and Dyna to the veterinarian, but the woman refused. At last, a man drove by, saw the scene, and stopped to help her. He got Carolyn and her three dogs into his car and drove as rapidly as possible to the nearest veterinarian. Dyna was rushed into emergency, and Carolyn waited with Toby and Andrea. She was covered with blood, and her other two dogs were pacing the waiting room, visibly upset.

Finally, the veterinarian came out and said that there was nothing more she could do for Dyna. The dog had been too badly injured to do anything for her, except help her die painlessly. She gently asked Carolyn what she wanted to do. There wasn't really a choice, as Dyna was suffering, so Carolyn and her two dogs went into the exam room and stood by Dyna's side as a lethal injection of pentobarbital was administered. Dyna died immediately, leaving Carolyn with memories that haunt her to this day.

I first spoke to Carolyn two months after the tragic incident. The veterinarian had been very concerned about Carolyn's state of mind that day and suggested that she call me, as she might need help dealing not just with the loss of Dyna, but also with the way in which the loss had occurred. At the time, Carolyn felt that she did not need help, and she didn't call.

But some time after Dyna's death she began to have horrible nightmares. It was at this point that she decided she might need some help. She phoned me one afternoon and told me her veterinarian had suggested she call. She stated that she didn't think she needed therapy, she just wanted her nightmares to go away. I asked her what the nightmares were about.

Then she told me her story. Her voice had a flat, monotonous quality, as if she were describing something that had happened to someone else. She said she needed to see me only to deal with her nightmares, as they were causing her to avoid sleeping, and this was affecting her job. At our first session she told me the story again, using the same, flat, monotone voice. She did not cry, even though she admitted that Dyna had been her favorite "child."

Carolyn was a single woman, living alone with her dogs; her nearest relatives were in New Jersey. She did have some friends on the teaching staff at the elementary school where she taught, but no one close. I noticed that she sat very stiffly, her body poised as if she would get up and bolt out of the office at any moment.

The only emotion she expressed outwardly was anger at the guardian of the dog that killed Dyna. She wondered what kind of person would let a dog do that to another "person." She said again that she was having horrible dreams about the event that woke her up, and she also admitted to having flashbacks of the attack, and to isolating herself from her friends. She said she was more irritable than normal, short with her students. and more fearful than she had been before the incident. She thought it odd that she hadn't cried since it happened, but she figured she must be okay since she hadn't. She did wish the disturbing dreams would go away, though.

As we finished the session it became clear to me that Carolyn was suffering from post-traumatic stress disorder (often called "PTSD"). I suggested that we meet a few more times to deal with her nightmares and perhaps anything else that might be bothering her. She agreed, and we saw each other once a week for several months. As you will learn, PTSD may not be entirely suitable for self-help work. It is a significant public health problem affecting millions of Americans. If untreated, it can last a lifetime.

Activity: Writing Down Your Losses

Before we get into the specifics of PTSD, perhaps you want to describe in your journal, or on your tape recorder, a trauma you have experienced that may have affected the course of your life. The trauma may or may not be related to your pet; however, since the subject of concern is pet loss, you are probably reading this chapter because you have experienced a traumatic loss of a pet. Do any of Carolyn's symptoms remind you of how you reacted? Or perhaps you experienced other symptoms. Write your symptoms down because you will learn that there are many symptoms of PTSD that Carolyn did not have. We will discuss all of them in this chapter. However, if doing this activity is too hard or too painful for you at this time, don't do it! You might want to read the chapter first, and, if you feel up to it, do the activity after you have read the chapter.

What Is Post-Traumatic Stress Disorder?

Defined simply, a *trauma* is a catastrophic stressor a person has experienced that falls outside the range of ordinary human experiences; one that would be a markedly distressing experience for anyone. Examples of trauma include rape; combat experiences; torture; assault; surviving a natural disaster, such as an earthquake or flood; seeing a friend, family member, or pet killed; or any number of other catastrophic events. You needn't actually witness firsthand a traumatic event; a vision or a vivid description of such an event can trigger a PTSD response.

Post-traumatic stress disorder is a severe response to trauma. It begins with a triggering event, such as witnessing, experiencing, or being threatened with serious danger—a danger so terrifying that it causes long-lasting fear, horror, and helplessness. For our purposes, we will discuss PTSD as it relates to seeing or somehow being involved with the traumatic death or loss of your companion animal. By definition, PTSD is characterized by the requirement that a person must have been traumatized by a catastrophic stressor that falls outside the range of the normal everyday stressors that people experience all the time. To meet the major criterion for a diagnosis of PTSD, the person's symptoms must have persisted for more than one month.

What Does PTSD Do to People?

Carolyn's story can help you understand how PTSD affects some people who have experienced the traumatic loss of a pet.

First, there must be a re-experiencing of the event in at least one of the following ways:

o   Recurrent and intrusive distressing recollections of the event. In Carolyn's case, she spent a part of each day reliving the event as if it had just taken place.

o   Recurrent, distressing dreams of the event. Carolyn reported recurring nightmares about how Dynamite had died.

o   A sudden behavior or feeling that the event is recurring right now.

o   Intense psychological distress at exposure to events that symbolize or resemble an aspect of the traumatic event, including anniversaries of the event, reading about, or seeing movies or hearing stories about the event. If, for example, you read Carolyn's story and had an intense reaction that was beyond sadness, you may be dealing with PTSD now, as it relates to your current situation.

Other Symptoms of PTSD

Other symptoms are caused by PTSD, too. See if any of these apply to your situation. Again, Carolyn's story is useful as a way of helping you to understand how and if PTSD applies to you.

o   Thoughts and memories about the event evoke such intense emotional and physiological reactions that the person makes an effort to avoid thinking, feeling, or even talking about the trauma. Remember that Carolyn's voice and actions did not indicate how much pain she was actually feeling. Her voice was flat, and she spoke in a monotone. She didn't cry or sob. This was her psyche's way of dealing with the intense pain she was actually feeling. Carolyn believed that if she could just forget about it or avoid activities, places, or people associated with the trauma, she would feel better.

o   Feeling detached from others. Carolyn admitted to isolating herself from her friends.

o   Unable to express feelings the way one did before the event. Carolyn had been a loving and expressive woman before the event. After it, she was unable to express how she felt in the way she had before the event took place.

o   Markedly diminished interest in significant activities that formerly gave pleasure to the person, such as music, sex, food, dancing, and so on.

In addition to these symptoms, there are certain other criteria to consider when PTSD is suspected. For a correct diagnosis of PTSD, two of the following symptoms must have been present for more than one month's time. You may want to review Carolyn's story again. These symptoms include the following:

o   Difficulty falling or staying asleep

o   Irritability or outbursts of anger

o   Difficulty concentrating

o   Hypervigilance. Remember how stiffly Carolyn sat in the psychologist's office. She sat as if she might run away at any moment. That is what is meant by *hypervigilance*.

o   Exaggerated startle response. In other words, noises or movements that might not have startled you, or startled you only mildly prior to the traumatic event, become even more startling.

o   Physiological reactivity when exposed to events similar to the trauma you suffered. For example, if you are watching television and an animal is being hunted, you might begin to tremble or shake as you did when you were traumatized by your experience.

Common Signs and Signals of a Stress Reaction

The severity and length of your reaction(s) to your stressor will dictate the best treatment for you. It's important for you to understand and acknowledge that PTSD does not always go away on its own, although it has been known to do that, too.

Post-traumatic stress disorder reveals itself in four ways:

Physical   Emotional

Cognitive   Behavioral

Sometimes, the emotional aftershocks (or stress reactions) appear immediately after the traumatic event; however, sometimes they may appear a few hours or a few days later. In some cases, weeks, or even months may pass before the stress reactions appear at all.

Remember, it is common, in fact quite normal, to experience emotional aftershocks when you have lived through a horrible event. But, if you have experienced any of these symptoms for one month or longer, you could indeed be suffering from PTSD. Furthermore, the more symptoms you have, the greater your need for professional assistance. While you read the following list, note how many symptoms apply to you:

Physical signs of a stress reaction include all or some of the following: chills, thirst, fatigue, nausea, fainting, twitching, vomiting, dizziness, weakness, chest pain, headaches, elevated blood pressure, rapid heart rate, muscle tremors, teeth grinding, visual difficulties, profuse sweating.

Cognitive signs may include confusion; nightmares; uncertainty; hypervigilance; suspiciousness; intrusive images; casting blame; poor problem solving; poor abstract thinking; diminished attention span; inability to concentrate; poor memory; disorientation of time, place, or person; heightened or lowered alertness; increased or decreased awareness of surroundings.

Emotional signs may include fear, guilt, grief, panic, denial, anxiety, agitation, irritability, depression, intense anger, apprehension, emotional shock, emotional outbursts, feeling overwhelmed, loss of emotional control, inappropriate emotional response.

Behavioral signs may include withdrawal, antisocial acts, inability to rest, intensified pacing, erratic movements, change in social activity, change in speech patterns, loss or increase of appetite, hyperalertness to environment, increased alcohol or drug consumption, change in usual communication style (for example, a once talkative person becomes quiet and withdrawn).

Activity: Keep a Record of Your Symptoms

In your journal, or with your tape recorder, make a list of all the symptoms listed above that you may be experiencing at this time. The hope is that this record will help you to begin to "get in touch" with what is going on within yourself, so that you will be better equipped to seek appropriate treatment.

What to Do When Trauma First Occurs

Here are some simple tools to use immediately after you first experience your traumatic event. These tools will not make your traumatic event seem any less tragic, but they may help you to cope with or allay the effects that PTSD can produce. Keep in mind that these tools work for some people but not for others; so don't give up if you find yourself "stuck" and unable to do the recommended tasks. If such is the case for you, you might want to consider seeking the help of a mental health professional.

o   Within the first 24 to 48 hours after the traumatic event, periods of appropriate exercise, alternated with relaxation, will alleviate some of the physical reactions.

o   Structure your time: keep busy.

o   Talk to people. Talking can be a powerful healing medicine. Try to find others to talk to who will accept the loss of your pet as a legitimate grievous loss and a traumatic event.

o   Avoid trying to numb your pain with overuse of alcohol, prescription medications, or other drugs.

o   Maintain as normal a schedule as possible.

o   Give yourself permission to feel bad, and share your feelings with others. Again, try to make sure that the people you share with are those who will be empathic to this kind of loss.

o   Don't make any big changes in your life. For example, it would not be a good time to quit your job or move to another city. You will just take yourself and all your feelings with you.

o   Do make as many daily decisions as possible. That will give you the sense of exerting some control over the events in your life. After a traumatic event, we often feel that we have no control at all. Doing this will help you realize you do indeed have some control.

o   Get plenty of rest. If you have problems sleeping, stay in bed for 20 minutes, then if you can't fall asleep, get up and go into another room. Read or watch television until you start to feel sleepy, then go back to bed. The reason for this exercise is that you don't want to associate not being able to sleep with your own bed. Such an association will make getting a good night's sleep harder in the future.

o   Recurring thoughts, nightmares, and flashbacks are normal. Don't try to fight them. They will decrease over time.

o   Eat well-balanced and regular meals, even if you don't feel like it.

You may be thinking that these ideas might work for others, but yours is a more complicated case. And indeed it may be.

The next section, Lauren's Story, is about another person I had the privilege of working with, whose story was both the same and different from Carolyn's. In both cases, they lost their dear companions, but Lauren's case had some markedly different components.

Lauren's Story

I first met Lauren in 1999, when she was nineteen years old. As she entered my office, I couldn't help noticing how she was dressed: she wore horseback riding boots, a belt with a turquoise buckle around her jeans, and her long, dark hair was pulled tightly back. Lauren had been on her way to becoming an Olympic competitor when her horse, Brew, was poisoned with oleander that had been mixed in with his hay. Oleander, a plant from the dogbane family, is highly toxic to both humans and animals. Brew was Lauren's "special" horse, and she couldn't get over his death. Her grief was compounded by the fact that her whole life had been centered on riding, and now she had no horse to ride. Her parents had sacrificed their own careers to take Lauren to riding events because in their eyes and the eyes of the equestrian world she had shown great promise.

Her experience was different from Carolyn's in several ways. First, she did not actually see her horse die of the poison. Instead, she had thoughts and images of the agony in which Brew might have died. Second, she "beat herself up" for not being there to oversee the buying of the hay. She believed that if she had been there, she might have been able to spot the oleander. She had been at a horse show, however, when the event occurred.

Third, she did not get the opportunity to try to "save" Brew from his terrible fate by just being there, even if she could not have prevented his death. And last, she did not get to say good-bye to him when he was dying. All of these regrets were having a profound effect on her ability to function. Her distress was further compounded by the fact that her whole world revolved around horses and riding, and now she felt exiled from that world. It was too painful for her to go to the shows and be with the friends who could have comforted her. She felt utterly alone.

When Lauren agreed to let me tell her story, she asked that I include her memorial to Brew. These are her words, and they became a great tool in her healing process.

Brew

*There was never a day that you let me down. I always
knew that no matter what, I could count on you. You
made it possible for me to achieve so many of my dreams
and made them a reality. Without you, I don't know where
I would be today. The day I lost you, a part of me died
with you. There is a hole in my heart. My heart breaks
each time I walk into the barn and you are no longer
there to greet me. From the Children's Hunters, where we
got our start, to the Equitation, the Jumpers and into the
Grand Prix, you were a champion, a one-in-a-million and
a once-in-a-lifetime horse. You gave me everything you
had, every time you set foot in the ring. When everyone
said you couldn't do it, we proved them wrong. We
believed in each other. We were a team. There will never
be another like you. Nothing can or will ever replace you.
Your shoes could never be filled. I will cherish you always.
I miss you every minute of the day. My world revolved
around you. I am so thankful for the nine years that we
were able to spend together. You were my best friend,
you were my life and you are my hero. I know that you
will be here to watch over me and help me through.
You touched my life and I will love you always.*

—Lauren

An important difference between Lauren's story and Carolyn's is
that Brew was more than a companion animal; he was an integral part
of Lauren's working life. For those of you not familiar with the equestrian world, there are many hoops and hurdles one must achieve to be
the best in each category. With this comes not only prestige in that
world, but financial compensation. When Brew died, Lauren lost both a
friend and a financial partner with whom she loved working. Even if she
had the money to buy a new horse, it would have taken her years to get
"in sync" with the new horse so that they could perform together.

Think of the ice skating pairs at the Olympics. They have practiced
years together for that one shining moment. If one or the other of the
pair breaks a leg or dies, it would be impossible to find another partner
who could perform in the same way without years of joint practice.
Lauren's horse was much like a service animal in that he helped Lauren
do what she wanted to do.

The concept is similar to Guide Dogs for the blind, Canine Companions for the disabled, or Hearing Dogs for the deaf. These are all

called service dogs. All these dogs help people to live a better quality of life than they would without the animal. When these animals die or must be taken out of service, for the person they were helping it is as if a part of their physical self is taken. This can present even greater psychological challenges than the loss of a companion animal that was not a service animal.

Both Carolyn and Lauren responded well to treatment, and they were both able to resume their normal lives, ridding themselves of the disturbing symptoms of PTSD. Lauren, in fact, eventually acquired a new horse, with which she developed a close bond, and she was able to resume her riding career. She will never forget Brew and the special relationship they shared, but because she successfully overcame PTSD, she was able to move ahead with her life.

Post-Traumatic Stress Disorder and Service Animals

Most of you have seen people who are accompanied by service animals, like those discussed above. These are animals who have been trained to help a human being to function better with the animal's help than without it. For example, blind people walking with a German shepherd beside them have a better sense of knowing where to walk, when to stop, and when to go. The animal, in effect, becomes the person's own eyes.

You may have also seen dogs who look like they are wearing backpacks around their middle. They are often seen accompanying people in wheelchairs. These are commonly known as Canine Companions for Independence, although there are other organizations that train this type of service animal, and they, too, allow the person to function better.

These dogs can turn lights on and off, pick up something that a person has dropped, and perform a variety of other tasks to make life easier for a disabled person. Again, they serve as replacements for nonfunctioning appendages.

Perhaps you have also seen or heard of what are called Hearing Dogs. These animals are trained to let a deaf person know when the phone or doorbell is ringing or when some other noise needs human attention. In this case, they become the ears for that person. As you can imagine, the human-animal bond in these relationships can be quite strong. These are more than exclusively companion animals because they add another dimension to the person's life that would not otherwise be there. They are working with that person to provide a better quality of life. In these situations, both human and animal can become quite attached to one another.

Since dogs are most commonly used for these functions, the bond can be even more intense. Wolves in the wild are pack animals, and dogs (which are descendants of wolves) are also pack animals. This means that if they are bonded to you, you become part of their pack and are usually considered the Alpha, or dominant, animal. They trust you to make the right decisions for your pack, even if it's just the two of you. You, in turn, often trust the dog with your life.

This is one of the reasons that when someone loses a service animal, it can be more traumatic than the loss of a companion animal. A person who loses a service animal also loses a certain sense of freedom enjoyed when the animal was alive. It's almost as if an appendage has been amputated. A loss of this nature can lead to post-traumatic stress disorder, even if the service animal did not die a violent or traumatic death.

An article published in *Anthrozoos,* a journal of the interactions between people and animals (Nicholson, Kemp-Wheeler, and Griffiths 1995), studied Guide Dog owners' experience of grief symptoms when they lost their dog. Many of the symptoms, such as reliving events, feeling very sad and low, numbness/emptiness, wanting to talk about their dog (or, conversely, being unable to talk about the dog), feeling like crying, anxiety, restlessness, unreality/out of touch with the world, dreaming about the dog, were all symptoms of post-traumatic stress disorder.

The authors make a point of saying that, in the past, the purpose of the Guide Dogs for the Blind Association was to provide blind people with dogs to enhance mobility, replacing each dog as it came to the end of its working life. Attention to the emotional consequences for the client when the relationship ends has not been traditionally recognized as part of the association's function. Fortunately, this is changing, as many organizations like Guide Dogs for the Blind are recognizing the intense emotional attachment that people can form with their service animals.

In other words, as a society, we are beginning to recognize that the human-animal bond can be experienced in varying degrees of intensity. Therefore, as with any death or separation, there are varying degrees of grief and there is no "right" way to grieve, nor is there an exact time when it should be over. However, as stated earlier, profound traumatic grief can leave you "stuck," and you may need additional tools to help you through it, particularly if the animal you lost was a service animal.

Let us now take a look at the different possible psychological treatments available for someone experiencing signs and symptoms of PTSD.

Psychological Treatments for PTSD

As we said at the beginning of this chapter, PTSD is a complicated disorder that is difficult to treat by self-help means alone. Therefore, we feel it is important to suggest that if you are experiencing the symptoms of PTSD, you might have a better chance for a positive outcome if you seek help from a mental health professional. These professionals include psychiatrists, psychologists, marriage and family therapists, and licensed clinical social workers. Make sure that when interviewing a potential therapist you ask if he or she has had experience working with PTSD.

If you are considering seeking professional help for your loss of a companion animal or service animal, make sure that the therapist understands this, and is comfortable dealing with PTSD caused by the loss of an animal. Some therapists are not animal lovers, nor do they appreciate the unique benefits of pet guardianship. They may not believe that your distress is really about the loss of your companion animal at all. Such a therapist would not be a good choice for you, because one of the most fundamental determinants of the effectiveness of therapy is the relationship between the therapist and the client.

You should feel at ease with this person, be able to tell this person anything and feel safe, and trust that this person can help you. If any of these elements are lacking, it might be better to look for another therapist. Interviewing a therapist in advance is always a good idea. If the therapist won't give you a few minutes of his or her time on the phone, so that you can learn a little about their psychological approach and what their focus of therapy includes, I would suggest you keep trying. It may be a little frustrating, but in the end it will be worth the effort. Just as no two people are alike, no two therapists have the same approach. You need to feel comfortable with whomever you decide to work. This cannot be emphasized enough, especially when it comes to issues surrounding pet loss.

Modes of Treatment

There are various approaches to treating PTSD. The following are a few of the most common psychotherapies used by mental health professionals. It is not within the scope of this book to describe all of the different approaches used to treat PTSD. The good news is that if one particular treatment does not work, the chances are good that there is another one that does. So try not to get discouraged if the first attempts do not achieve the results you want and deserve.

Cognitive Behavioral Therapy

Cognitive behavioral therapy addresses the thoughts and beliefs generated by the traumatic event. The therapy focuses on how people with PTSD have interpreted the traumatic event with respect to their appraisals about the world and themselves. You might want to review chapter 4, where the group discussion illustrates a form of cognitive therapy.

Exposure Therapy

This form of therapy asks the client, basically to re-experience the traumatic event by using visualization and repeated narrations. The therapist may ask you to close your eyes and visualize what happened. You are then asked to rate the level of your subjective distress on a scale of 10–100: 10 is no distress, 100 is the most fear you could experience. The goal is that, through repeated "exposure" to the traumatic event, you will achieve a progressive reduction in your distress numbers.

Biofeedback and Relaxation Training

Biofeedback and relaxation training alone are ineffective treatments for PTSD. If they are used, it must be in conjunction with another therapy. However, they are very effective as anxiety-management techniques while you are working on PTSD.

Relaxation training teaches you to relax to help control your anxiety. This provides a skill set and some tools that will help you to tolerate the other therapy that you might employ to treat PTSD. Biofeedback is a process designed to help you reduce tension and anxiety. Through this technique, you acquire quite a bit of information about your own physiological processes. Success is measured by reductions in heart rate, muscle tension, or other physiological processes.

Eye Movement Desensitization and Reprocessing (EMDR)

Eye movement desensitization and reprocessing—frequently used as a treatment for PTSD—is a technique that uses simultaneous physical and thought processes. The goal is to increase the psychological strength of positive thoughts and reduce the psychological strength of the traumatic experience. Clinicians use many variations of EMDR techniques, so if you're considering it as an option, ask the clinician to describe to you exactly how the process works.

There are many more treatments used to deal with PTSD, but these seem to be the most helpful for the greatest number of people.

Remember that if one of these doesn't work, there are many others, and the chances are very high that you will be able to find the appropriate psychotherapy for yourself.

Post-traumatic stress disorder does not have to ruin your life, no matter how traumatic the event. You *can* feel better, and your companion would want that for you. If you can't do this for yourself, perhaps you can do it for your friend, who was so much a part of your life. After all, the bond goes both ways. You want what's best for your companion animal, and your pet wants what's best for you. Helping yourself, therefore, helps the animal. Your companion may not be with you anymore in a physical body, but it may be with you in spirit, and it would want you to take care of yourself. If you think you are suffering from PTSD, please get the help you need. It is available and you are worth it!

Chapter 8

Mommy, Where Did Buddy Go?

Oh where, oh where, has my little dog gone?
Oh where, oh where, can he be?
With his ears cut short and his tail cut long,
Oh where, oh where, can he be?

—Traditional children's song

Nine-year-old Jimmy sat stoically beside his chronically ill mother in the pet-loss support group. She had brought him because he had not cried once since his new kitten had accidentally been run over by a car. He had loved this kitten, and his mother was surprised by his lack of emotion.

The group consisted of eight adults and Jimmy. As usual, I discussed the grieving process and then asked each member to tell his or her story. I decided to let Jimmy go last. As the first person spoke, all members of the group began to cry—all except Jimmy. He sat there, eyes downcast, his body rigid. After all the adults had shared their story, I asked Jimmy if he would like to tell his. He stared at me for a moment and then began to share.

As soon as he began, he started sobbing as if something inside of him had finally let go. It took him a long time to tell his story because he couldn't seem to stop crying long enough to continue. When he was finished, I asked him why he had not cried before and why he felt he could cry now.

Jimmy replied, "I have to be strong for my mother and younger sisters, and I thought it was probably silly to cry for a cat. But when I saw the grown-ups cry, I knew it was okay."

We all thanked him for telling us his story and asked if he felt any better. He said yes and thanked the group for helping him to know it was okay to cry for an animal.

Jimmy's story is not unique. He is one of many children who share or have shared the love of a pet and who cannot grieve for it when it dies, because they believe that grieving is stupid, or that the adults in their world don't care. Jimmy was lucky to have a mother who did understand and made the effort to get him the help that he wanted and needed to get through his pain.

For many children, losing a pet is a profoundly painful experience. This chapter is about helping children through the pain of the loss of a companion animal. The relationships children develop with these animal are often different from adult relationships with animals, and, thus, the way they deal with the loss of a pet may be different, too. The information in this chapter should enable you to better help your child, or any child, cope with the loss of a special friend.

Childhood Teachers

My first companion animal was a calico cat named Bibsy. I got her when I was five years old. Bibsy followed me everywhere, much like a dog. There was a field behind our house that the kids in the neighborhood were not allowed to play in, as it was dangerous. Naturally, it was our favorite place to play. Unfortunately, Bibsy always followed us and we usually got in trouble.

One day, I got the idea to lock Bibsy in a closet so we could go play in the field. We had a great play day, and I came in for our usual 6:00 dinner. During dinner my mom asked, "Where's Bibsy?" Of course I knew, but I had a feeling that neither she nor my father would be pleased with Bibsy's current accommodations. I lied and said, "I don't know." Big mistake! Almost immediately, Bibsy let out a cry of dismay, alerting my parents to her whereabouts. They let her out and then suggested that I go to my room and think about what I had done.

"How would you feel," they asked, "if we locked you in a closet?"

Bibsy followed me to my room. As I sat on my bed, feeling bad, she jumped up beside me and started purring. She had forgiven me, and all was right again. I remember thinking, if only people were this forgiving. I told her I would never do that to her again, and I think she knew I was sorry.

I used to tell Bibsy secrets that I wouldn't share with anyone. I learned a great deal from this wonderful feline: compassion, empathy, forgiveness, and love. As I think back, at that time she was my best friend.

She died when she was eight years old. Bibsy taught me the value of love and friendship, and I will always remember her as the special teacher that she was.

I wouldn't be surprised if the story of my relationship with Bibsy stirs familiar feelings in you. Perhaps you were close to a companion animal when you were a child, or maybe your own child or children are very attached to their pets. Many of life's lessons involving loyalty, trust, love, compassion, and empathy are more easily learned by children when a beloved pet is doing the teaching. Animals have a remarkable capacity for such traits, and children seem to be particularly attuned to what a companion animal can show them. Often it's easier for children to learn from animals than from adults—the lessons seem clearer and more definable on a childlike level. Perhaps it's because our pets never really grow up in the same sense that human beings do. They usually stay childlike until the end of their lives, and children can relate better to them because of that quality.

Here's another example. There is a farm in Brewster, New York, called Green Chimney's (Caras 1997). It's not an ordinary farm but a special school for troubled children from New York's inner cities. They learn skills they might not learn at home or in traditional schools. This amazing place was founded by a man named Sam Ross. When Sam was a young adult he had an idea. He would create a school for young kids, in a farm setting, and the kids would care for the animals. As a young man, Ross had a special affinity for animals, and he thought that "lost" children might benefit from the teachings of these wise creatures.

Charles came to Green Chimney's as a troubled thirteen-year-old who had problems dealing with anger. When he arrived, he connected almost immediately with a horse named Warlock. This is what Charles says:

> You can tell they're sweet by their eyes. I like to look at their eyes because I know they see me, too. You can tell how horses feel by reading their ears. If they lay their ears back, they're angry or something is bothering them. If their ears stick straight up they are wondering about something. When they put their ears forward they are happy. I don't like it when they are angry or upset about things.

He went on, "They listen to me. Horses like being around kids; they like it when I'm with them. They especially like it when I pet them. It makes me feel better, too. I would never take my anger out on a horse."

Charles' story is especially important because there is a direct relationship between childhood cruelty to animals and aggressive behavior toward humans in adulthood. Research suggests that if a child can learn to be kind toward animals, he or she may develop empathy that may later be translated into compassion as an adult (Lockwood and Ascione 1997). We know that anger often leads to aggression, so as Charles learns the value of empathy toward Warlock, ideally, as he gets older, he will not take his anger out on adults.

Activities: Learning in Pets and Children

1. Ask your child to think of all of the things that he or she learned from the pet, for example, responsibility, love, and friendship.

2. Ask your child what the pet learned. (Maybe your child taught the pet a trick.) This will help the child remember that the relationship was good for both of them.

Animals as Therapists

Eight-year-old Rose was brought to my office by her mother, Terry. For the last six months Rose had been experiencing what she described as "worries." Her teachers thought it would be a good idea for Terry to take her to a psychologist. Rose's worries sometimes spiraled into panic attacks so severe that she could hardly breathe. The panic attacks happened both at school and at home. When asked, Rose said she mostly worried about "getting into trouble," either with a teacher or another child.

Rose's family consisted of two-parents, a ten-year-old brother, three cats, and two dogs. Both parents loved animals, as did Rose. Her favorite was her dog Daisy. After talking to Rose it became clear that she was very connected to Daisy. I decided that Daisy might be a helpful part of the therapy, so I asked Rose to bring Daisy to the next session.

As we talked, she petted her dog and I asked her how it felt to do that. She said it made her feel calm, and she didn't worry when she petted Daisy. She liked stroking the soft fur. For the next session, I asked Rose to bring a picture of Daisy along with her school binder. We put Daisy's picture on the cover of the binder, and I suggested that when she worried at school she could look at Daisy, and remember how calm she felt when she was petting her.

The following week, Rose and her mother reported that she had done a lot better, and had had no panic attacks. Rose said that when she started to worry, she looked at the dog's picture and remembered what it felt like to stroke Daisy's soft fur. This calmed her, and she was pleased that she was getting better. The power of the connection between the child and the animal was therapeutic for Rose, and she is now doing very well, with few or no "worries."

Every week volunteers from the San Diego Humane Society load up kennels and carriers with special dogs, cats, puppies, kittens, rabbits, guinea pigs, and rats. They take these animals to visit with the children at various schools, adolescent psychiatric wards, and day care centers. The purpose of these visits is to provide animal contact to children and adolescents who may not otherwise get a chance to pet or bond with a companion animal. According to the volunteers, just the smiles on the children's faces are worth the effort.

For a brief while, the children can forget their problems, and focus on the joy animals can bring into the lives of human beings. They play with the animals, stroke their fur and cuddle with them. Laughter and play are the order of the day. Both animals and children seem to enjoy this interaction, and the special chemistry between them is clearly observable.

Activity: "What Do You Like Most About Your Pet?"

Ask your children what is the thing they like most about their pet or pets. It may be that they make them laugh, which we all know is good therapy, or that they are their best friends. Whatever the response may be, it will be helpful for your children to recognize and acknowledge the pet's importance in their lives.

Special Relations, Special Reactions

Children often have a very different relationship with their companion animal than the adults who also may share in that animal's life. To help a child deal with the loss of a pet, it may be helpful to understand the differences in these relationships.

In the course of my work with the human-animal bond, I am often asked to speak at elementary schools on the benefits of having pets. Almost as soon as I begin, the students jump right into the conversation. It seems that when it comes to talking about their pets, they are not as shy or inhibited as they might be with other subjects.

Over the years, I have taken notes on what these children say about their companion animals. The quotes that follow come from fourth- and fifth-grade elementary students over a period of ten years. It's interesting to note that, almost without exception, the children have pets, even those from areas that would be defined as economically disadvantaged. The animals vary, from dogs, cats, hamsters, and fish to mice, snakes, iguanas, and horses. One student had a goat.

One of the most universal comments is, "My pet is my best friend." I've heard this comment in every classroom I have ever spoken to, and usually about half the room will agree to the truth of the statement.

Here are some other common revelations:

I tell my pet secrets that I wouldn't tell anyone else.

I play with my pet every day. He is more fun than most people.

My pet understands me. No one else understands me the way he does.

I like sleeping with my pet. It makes me feel safe.

I like it when he gets into trouble with my parents. I don't feel like it's always me. Then I usually hug him and tell him it's okay, I love him.

In one classroom, the children were arguing about who got to take the class's pet hamster home for the weekend. One young boy spoke softly and said, "I would really like to take him home this weekend because my dad just died, and I feel all alone." Almost instinctively, the other students empathetically understood the comfort the hamster would be able to provide for their classmate, and the class agreed that he should be the one to take care of the hamster.

Douglas, a fourth-grader, sat in class wearing a back brace. He had fallen off his horse and had fractured several vertebrae. This is what he said about his horse, Gallant: "It wasn't his fault that I fell. I wasn't paying attention to what I was doing. I hope my parents don't get rid of him. I am afraid of that because I love him so much. He is my best friend."

As you can see by these comments and circumstances, children often have a very close connection to their companion animals. When they lose these friends, they may have a different kind of grieving experience, depending on the age of the child. This may also be the child's first experience with death, so it's important that you, as the adult, know what to say and how to say it.

Activity: What Is Special About Your Pet?

Ask the children in your life what is special about their pet. You may want to begin to keep a scrapbook of the important events in the pet's life with the family. Help the children write down the answers to these questions: What kind of pet was it? When was the pet born? How did the pet come to live with them? What was his or her name, and how did it come to have that name? Did the pet have nicknames? What did the pet like and not like (to eat, to do, etc.)?

Child Development

Before we delve into the specifics of a child's grieving experience, you might want to know more about how a child's mind develops when it comes to understanding certain concepts, such as death. The stages of development are explained in Wolman's *Handbook of Developmental Psychology* (1982).

Babies (up to two years of age) can sense when stress levels escalate in families, but they are not aware of the cause of the tension. They do not understand the concept of death in any way, but they will understand that there is tension. Babies can best be reassured by hugs, laughter, and keeping routines as normal as possible.

Toddlers and preschoolers (two to five years) understand that the loss of a pet is a significant event, but they do not understand the permanence of death. They may miss their playmate and ask questions, but, typically, they don't grieve for a long period of time over the loss. One of the ways I approach this age group when trying to explain why Fido won't be coming home is to say something like, "Remember your toy that broke, and you couldn't play with it anymore? That's what happened to Fido. His body broke and the doctor couldn't fix him, so he won't be with us anymore." That explanation often works well with this age category. They understand that concept, much more easily than a lengthy discussion about death.

Young school-age children (six to eight years) often personify death, thinking of it as a monster or the Grim Reaper. They imagine death in a concrete way, but believe that it is possible to hide from it or avoid it. Because of this belief, young children may feel angry that their pet died. They wonder why it didn't just run away or avoid death, because then it would still be with them. They also might believe that, in some way, they are responsible for the pet's death. It is important for you, the adult, to reassure your child that he or she is not responsible, and that Fido could not hide nor avoid death. You may have to reassure your child of this many times.

Children of this age may regress to younger levels of functioning when a pet dies. Bedwetting, thumb sucking, or tantrums, all long gone from their behavior, might reoccur. Knowing this, you should continue to be there for your children and continually reassure them that they didn't cause the pet's death. Punishment or humiliation for any regressive behavior tends only to make matters worse, possibly even causing the children to become "stuck" in the unwanted behavior.

Older school-age children (eight to twelve years) usually know that death is permanent and not reversible. This may be their first experience with the death of someone they loved. You can help by being supportive and letting the child know it's okay to cry or be sad about the loss. You can further help by actually saying that you, too, are sad, and that it's normal to feel sad in these circumstances. This is also a good time to talk about death and the grieving process.

Adolescents (thirteen to seventeen years) often go back and forth between wanting to be treated like an adult one day, and wanting to be treated like a child the next. Therefore, it is no surprise that on some days the teenager will be devastated by the death of his or her companion animal, and on another day say, "It's not a big deal." However, teens often grieve the most deeply over the loss of a pet, because that animal may have been with them their entire life. They may miss the everyday routine of having this pet in their lives. Still, they are trying to be adults, so they might not let an adult know how much they hurt.

It is up to the adult to be watchful for any change in teenagers' behavior patterns, as they may not talk about their grief. Such changes might be withdrawal, sleeping difficulties, or acting out in inappropriate ways that are different from the normal behavior of the teen. During this time, teens should be treated in much the same way you would treat younger children. You should offer to spend time with them, share feelings, and discuss questions about the loss.

Now that you have learned the various ways in which children of different ages might react to the death of their companion animals, you will more effectively understand what a child experiences in this situation. With that understanding you will be more effective in helping your child or children through the grieving process.

Helping Children with the Loss of a Companion Animal

For many children, the loss of a companion animal is their first experience with death and bereavement. Often the pet is the child's first personal friend to die. In fact, one important aspect of pet guardianship for children is that it provides the child with experience in dealing with the realities of illness and death, which will help prepare them for these experiences later in life. By fully experiencing the grief of losing a pet, the child learns that death is a natural part of the life process. It is emotionally painful, but it is tolerable and does not last forever.

There is a tendency, however, to minimize a child's grief over a lost pet. In the vast literature on children and bereavement, there are few references to the bereavement that children undergo from the loss of a pet. For many children, the death of a pet is a profound experience and should be recognized as such. Following are some general guidelines on how to help your child deal with this profound loss.

1. **Tell the truth**. If your pet was euthanized, don't say it was put to sleep or ran away. Imagine a child who has been told that his or her pet was put to sleep. Suppose that a few months later the child has to have surgery and the anesthesiologist says, "We're going to put you to sleep for a while." The child may

panic because when Fido was "put to sleep," he never came back. It is better to say, "Fido died peacefully and without pain." If the child asks what "dead" means, you might say, "The animal's body stops working and won't be able to be with us anymore."

If you tell a child that the pet ran away, the child possibly could feel rejected or abandoned, or even go searching for the lost pet, hoping for its return. He or she might think, "I'm not even lovable enough for my cat to stay with me." Talking to a child about euthanasia should be done in such a way that the child can understand; again, according to the appropriate developmental stage that the child's age entails.

If the pet was run over, explain that it was a horrible accident, and that it wasn't the child's fault. Truth is important because if children find out they have been lied to, they may not trust you to tell the truth in the future.

2. **Ask children if they have any questions**. They may have none or many. Again, be as age appropriate as possible when giving answers, but answering is important. Don't brush it off and say, "Forget about it, it was only a dog. It's in the past, let's move forward."

3. **Explain that being sad or angry is normal**. You might want to let them know that you feel sad and angry, too, and that together you will get through this hard time. It can be a wonderful time to be together as a family and talk about the lost companion. Making a scrapbook or a drawing of the animal can help. A memorial of some kind is also useful, for both children and adults. If you have videos of your companion animal, watching them might be helpful, although you should count on tears. Explain, again, that tears are okay when we lose someone we love.

4. **Let the children say good-bye to the pet, if possible**. This allows the first step of the grieving process to begin. Ask them if they want to see the body, and respect their wishes. Some children may not want to and others will. Let it be up to the child. However, if the pet had a particularly gruesome death, for example, being run over by a car, it may not be a good idea for the younger children (or even some older ones) to see the body. You might explain that Rover wouldn't want you to see him this way. Be sure to have a memorial service, even without the body. Let the children write a poem or say

something about their pet, for example, all of the things that they loved about the pet. It's important not to make the child do anything if he or she doesn't want to do whatever you suggest. Some children need to process grief quietly in their own way. Remember there are no right or wrong ways to grieve. The important thing is to give the child a chance to grieve. Children may end up with guilty thoughts if they think they have not grieved enough.

5. **Ask them how they are feeling about the loss**. You might have to help younger children find the words to describe how they are feeling. With older children, you might have to watch for behavioral signs, as they sometimes do not want to express their feelings to adults. Keep trying, however, as older children often need to talk the most.

6. **Inform others of what is going on in your child's life**. Ask neighbors, teachers, relatives, or friends for extra support and understanding of your child right now. Ask them to help in keeping a watchful eye on your child in this sad and difficult time. Remember, sometimes behaviors may change, and others will be able to help you see these changes.

7. **Don't put time limits on your child's grief**. Remember that we all grieve in different ways, and for some the grieving process goes on longer than for others. If your child doesn't seem to be getting better after about three to six months, you might want to consult a mental health professional.

8. **Don't tell children more than they want to know about losing the pet**. Even though you want to be honest, don't give every detail, unless they ask. Sometimes too much information can overload a child, and make the grieving process more difficult.

9. **If your child wishes to have a memorial of some kind, respect his or her wishes**. Such rituals are a final act of reconciliation to the departure of a loved one. They may be as simple as saying a few words about the pet, or as elaborate as staging a formal funeral service. Remember, you don't have to have the body to do this. Pictures will work just as well.

10. **Don't try to get another pet too soon**. Let the children have the time to work through the grieving process so that

they (and you) might heal. If you do get another companion animal right away, it's best to avoid getting the same breed of dog or the same color of cat because your children will probably expect the same behaviors from these new animals, and they will be disappointed. Just as no two people are alike, no two animals are alike.

Above all, remember that the mentally healthy way of dealing with grief is not denial of the tragedy, but the frank acknowledgment of a painful separation. For those of us who have loved and lost our companion animals, and this includes children, it is a painful and emotional experience. However, it can also be a time of sharing with your children and teaching them about life, love, and death.

The Pet Attachment Worksheet for Children

The Pet Attachment Worksheet for Children is designed to help adults understand the attachment the child had with his or her companion animal. Unlike the adult Pet Attachment Worksheet, there are no cut-off scores to indicate levels of bonding. The more "yes" scores, the more the attachment. If you have more than one child, you may find that each had a different relationship with the pet. This will be helpful in determining which child may need a little more support from you.

You may also want to use the Pet Attachment Worksheet for Children as a way of talking about the pet. It can be used as a way to have a conversation with your children about the answers that they give to each of the questions.

Pet Attachment Worksheet for Children

Please write Y for "yes" or N for "no" to answer the following questions. (There are no right or wrong answers.)

1. Did you often talk to your pet? __

2. Did you tell your pet secrets that you wouldn't tell anyone else? __

3. Did you consider your pet a member of your family? __

4. Did you talk to your pet about your problems? __

5. Did your pet understand you when you're sad or feeling bad? __

6. Did you sleep with your pet, or would you have, if you could have? ____

7. Did you teach your pet certain tricks? ____

8. Were you proud of your pet? ____

9. Was your pet your best friend? ____

10. Did you celebrate your pet's birthday? ____

11. Did your pet participate in holiday events such as Christmas? ____

12. Did you buy gifts for your pet? ____

13. Do you have a drawing or picture of your pet? If so, is it special to you? ____

14. Do you miss your pet a lot? ____

15. Would you like another pet? ____

As you have seen, children have special needs when dealing with the loss of a companion animal. I hope that while reading this chapter you gained valuable information that will help you to provide the proper amount of attention and care in helping your child or children through the grieving process when they lose a pet.

The next chapter will take an in-depth look at a situation that no one ever anticipates but one that arises more often than you might think: circumstances that force you to give up a companion animal. Should you find yourself in that unfortunate position, the various options available to you are examined, along with the feelings of sadness and grief that go hand in hand with having to give up a beloved pet.

Chapter 9

Changing Circumstances

Grant me the serenity to accept the things I cannot change, courage to change the things I can, and the wisdom to know the difference.

—Serenity Prayer

Benjamin Franklin once said that the only two things certain in life were death and taxes. If Mr. Franklin were living today, I wonder if he wouldn't add a third certainty: *change.* We live in an age that has seen enormous technological and scientific advances. Even though we enjoy the benefit of these advances, along with them comes increased pressure on us to adapt, at perhaps a faster rate than the human psyche has ever had to do before. Stress, anxiety, and depressive disorders are on the rise. This, I believe, is partly due to the pressures of our fast-paced society.

There was a time when we could count on working for a company thirty years and retire with a gold watch, health benefits, and a pension. Today, many of us are compressed into little office cubicles, wondering when the next round of layoffs will begin. Sometimes, we must move to a new geographical location just to keep our jobs or to search for new ones. Families are split apart so that they can survive or better themselves. The elderly are put into nursing homes or senior citizen complexes, rather than living out their lives, as they once did, with their families. Because of these reasons and many other life changes, we are not always able to keep our beloved companion animals. If we move, it is not always easy to find a place that will allow pets. If we have to move abroad, many factors come into play, for example, lengthy quarantines. Sometimes, new circumstances are not good for pets or people. Seniors often find that they cannot take their pets with them to their new living situations. And yet, their pets may be their most beloved companions.

In this chapter we will look at the different circumstances that might force you to give up your pet. Having to give up a beloved companion animal can generate emotions that are difficult to deal with, perhaps on a par with the grief you would experience if your pet had died. We will try to provide ways to help you through this change.

Pets and the Elderly

The loss of a pet can be devastating for anyone, but for seniors it can be even more tragic. One reason is that the pet may represent the "last link" to another family member, such as a spouse. The pet may have lived with both husband and wife, and when the pet dies, memories may resurface of the departed loved one and the times that were shared together. Another reason may be that the pet is the only living connection that the person still has, and losing it leaves the person lonely and isolated.

I saw an illustration of this recently in the obituary section of the *Los Angeles Times* (Feb. 3, 2002) The obituary stated that Dolores

Gilstrap Powers passed away on December 1, 2001. After giving a brief description of her life, it said, "She is survived by her six beloved cats: Cliff, Samba, Tiger Lily, Sonny, Blondie, and Maybelline. Donations may be made in her memory to the Humane Society of America." It would appear that in Ms. Powers' case, the only family she had, or at least that she considered she had, was her six cats. She obviously must have been very close to them, and one might guess that they if they had died first, she would have been devastated.

Why might an elderly person be more attached than others to a companion animal? First, pets provide companionship, love, and touch that an older person might not get otherwise. The elderly are frequently isolated and spend a lot of time alone. A companion animal can fill the void left by the human beings who are no longer living or have moved away. For an older person, this void can create intense loneliness, which is often relieved by a companion animal. They know their pets aren't going anywhere!

Pets also can provide safety for older people, who often live alone. They know that a barking dog will likely scare away potential intruders. Beyond the safety issue, though, pets give them something to take care of and to care about, and through their pets the elderly may rekindle their sense of purpose in life. If they are isolated from their loved ones, pets will provide at least one living creature that they can be close to. Humans are programmed, along with other mammals, to want or even need the physical sensation of touch. Companion animals can provide this, and we can give it back to them.

When an elderly person loses a companion animal, he or she may become clinically depressed. This depression can lead to them not eating and sleeping as well as they should, and eventually to serious health issues. For some older people, walking the dog may have been the only thing that got them out of the house or provided any form of exercise. Perhaps you've read one of the many articles written in recent years citing research that has shown companion animals can lower blood pressure, cholesterol levels, and stress levels (Beck and Katcher 1996). All of these are particularly important as a person ages, so when an elderly person loses a companion animal he or she is, in a sense, losing a natural and healthy form of medication.

How Seniors Can Cope with Pet Loss

So, if you are elderly, what should you do if you lose or have to give up your companion animal? Here are some of the ideas that seniors have come up with in my pet-loss support groups. They speak from experience.

o   Grieve the loss of your companion and perhaps all of the other losses you have experienced that may be triggered by this loss. Refer to chapters 3 and 4 if you need tools for grieving or an explanation of the grieving process.

o   If possible, get another pet. Perhaps an older pet would be good so that you might not worry so much about your companion outliving you, as many seniors do. Humane societies and animal control shelters usually have many older pets. They are harder to adopt because most people want puppies and kittens. You would be helping another animal find a home as well as gaining the advantage of a new companion for yourself. Usually, these pets are already housebroken, vaccinated, and spayed or neutered. In some parts of the country, there are programs for seniors that allow you to adopt a pet for free. These programs sometimes provide free veterinary care and food for your new friend. Check with your local humane society or animal control shelter.

o   If you have a local animal shelter, humane society, or rescue organization in your area, perhaps you can volunteer your services there. The people who operate these organizations are always looking for volunteers to help take care of the animals, and your services would be greatly appreciated. Imagine how gratifying it would be to see and care for dozens of animals each day who are always happy to see you.

o   If you have to move into a facility that does not allow your pet to be with you, ask family, friends, or neighbors if they will take your companion. This way you could possibly still get to see your friend occasionally. However, make the attempt to find a facility that will take your pet before you give up. More and more senior facilities are letting people keep their companion animals as the people who run these facilities begin to appreciate the value of allowing seniors to have their pets' company.

o   If you can't find anyone to take your companion animal, perhaps you could find a foster home for it. This would be a home where you would allocate funds to a person or animal hospital to take care of your pet for the remainder of its natural life. This could be set up as a trust fund by an attorney. In the event that you pass before your animal does, you could also establish a trust fund for the care of your companion animal in your will.

o If you have to move into a senior citizen home, or a nursing or convalescent care facility, and cannot have your own pet, you might ask the administrator if there could be a resident communal pet that could live at the facility. Cats, birds, hamsters, and small animals make excellent communal pets, provided they are screened by an animal behaviorist to be sure that they are temperamentally suited for this kind of "position." This would allow all residents who want to be a part of this animal's life a chance to share the joy of pet guardianship. It also would give you a chance to meet your neighbors, as you would all have something in common. If the administrator does not agree to this, perhaps he or she would agree to have pet visitations by such organizations as the Humane Society or certain animal rescue groups. These organizations bring different pets to visit, usually once a week, and you can get your "fur fix" at least some of the time.

Ruth, an eighty-nine-year-old woman who recently moved into a skilled nursing facility, had never been a pet person. Much to her dismay, the facility had two resident cats who had the run of the building and loved to check in with all the patients several times a day. During the first few weeks, as Ruth was settling in, she complained mightily about the "pesky" cats who kept bothering her. After she had been there about a month, though, when I visited her, I would often find one of the cats curled up asleep on her bed. Ruth would caution me to speak quietly because I might wake up the cat and it would start pestering her. Soon, however, she gave up the pretense and asked me to bring kitty treats and toys whenever I visited. Both cats had eased their way into Ruth's heart, and they made her time at the facility much more pleasant.

o Attend a pet-loss support group or see a psychologist if you are having a lot of psychological difficulty with the loss of your companion animal. Remember, Medicare pays for seeing a psychologist, so don't be afraid to use your benefits if needed.

If you are comfortable using a computer and have access to the Internet, you might want to join in a chat room or discussion group with other bereaved persons. There is a list of Internet sites in the Resources section at the back of this book.

What If My Pet Outlives Me?

Earlier I mentioned the death of pet guardian Dolores Gilstrap Powers, who left behind six surviving cats. I hope Ms. Powers had instructions or a directive in place to take care of her companions in case of her death. Sometimes we don't always think of doing this; we simply assume our pets will die before we do. However, no matter what age you are, there is a possibility that your companion animal will outlive you. So to be on the safe side, it's best to have some kind of trust or will drawn up so that your companion will be taken care of if you are the first to die.

This document should be prepared by an attorney, so there will be no misunderstanding as to what your wishes are. In this will or trust, you should name a guardian, preferably someone familiar with your pet, to act in case you are physically incapacitated or are no longer living.

Obviously this person needs to agree beforehand to assume guardianship of your pet or pets. If you don't know someone willing to take on this task, you can also direct your executor to place your pet temporarily with a professional pet sitter, kennel, or animal hospital, and to authorize payment of the necessary fees while the executor tries to find a suitable home for your pet.

The language of the document will be provided by your attorney, but it might look something like the following:

> I bequeath my three cats, Kali, Bosco, and Tara, to Rose Brown. Rose Brown will act as guardian for my cats and will provide for the care and maintenance of them until they die. A trust fund to provide for their care is established, and that trust fund shall be administered by Rose Brown.

Further provisions can be specified, such as how you want their bodies disposed of when they die, or what your designated guardian should do in case he or she can no longer take care of your companions.

The document should be placed in a safe-deposit box with a copy maintained at your attorney's office. Along with the document, you should have medical records, the name of your veterinarian, any medications the pet needs, a description of your pet's temperament, what your pet likes to eat and play with, any nicknames your pet has and the date of its birth. If you have more than one pet, this should be done for each one.

Although many people never think to do this, I have heard over and over from pet guardians that once they have this document in place, they no longer worry about what will happen to their companion if something does happen to them. It is a comforting relief, no matter what age you happen to be.

Moving and Companion Animals

In these times of corporate downsizing, layoffs, high rents, and soaring housing costs, many of us are finding that we have to move, either to a different location in our own geographical area, to a different part of the state, or even to a different part of the country to find employment or affordable housing. Sometimes people must relocate to a public housing development, an apartment complex, or a rental house that prohibits pets. If this is your situation, you might find that you cannot keep your companion animal with you.

As you might imagine, this causes great distress for pet guardians. And although the prospect is almost unthinkable, certain circumstances might force you to relinquish your companion. It should be comforting to know, however, that you might be able to do something ahead of time. This is where knowing what the laws state regarding companion animals can be helpful.

Pets and the Law

Before giving up your pet because you have to move, you may want to consult the laws concerning pets in your state, or the state or county where you are moving. As an example, following are some of the laws in California, and they may give you an idea of what the laws are in *your* state with regard to pet guardianship. These laws are summarized from the *California Animal Laws Handbook* (2000).

o   Every individual with a disability has the right to be accompanied by a guide dog, signal dog, or service dog, especially trained for its particular purpose. This is in accord with the Americans with Disabilities Act of 1990. This means that a landlord or business owner cannot ban a service animal from living with you or being at work with you. You cannot be required to pay an extra charge or security deposit for the guide dog, service dog, or signal dog. If you have a problem with a landlord or other persons regarding your service dog, file a complaint with the Department of Fair Employment and Housing. *This is a national law.*

o   In California, no public agency that owns and operates rental housing accommodations can prohibit the keeping of not more than two pets by an elderly person or person requiring supportive services in the rental housing accommodations. For the purposes of this law, elderly refers to any person over sixty years of age. "Pet" refers to a domesticated dog, cat, bird, or aquarium. "Public" means state, county, city, and county, or other political subdivision of the state.

o   In California, the law prohibits mobile home parks and condominium associations from banning pets. This law allows the owners of mobile homes, condominiums, and other common interest developments to keep at least one dog, cat, bird, fish or other animal that lives in an aquarium. There can be reasonable rules established for pets by the mobile home parks and condominiums, so make sure you know what they are before deciding to move in. For example, some associations allow pets only under twenty pounds. That won't work if you have a seventy-pound Labrador.

If you move to Hawaii, you should know that there is a six-month quarantine on pets moving into the state. This means that you will have to board your companion for six months at a state-approved facility. For some pets, this can produce very strong feelings of abandonment, isolation, and general malaise. For others, it is not a particular problem. You know your pet's temperament better than anyone, so you will have to be the judge of how well you think your pet could handle being quarantined. Ask your veterinarian if you need more specifics or details regarding this particular situation and how it might apply to your pet.

If you don't think your pet would handle this well, you might reconsider your move, or if you absolutely must move, you may want to leave your pet behind with friends or family. Perhaps Hawaii will change its laws in the future, so check before you move.

All animal lovers hope there will be more allowances for companion animals by property owners in the future, but for now, there are at least a few that always must be observed. Always ask about the particular place you are moving to. You may be surprised that a lot of landlords who say "no pets" will be somewhat flexible, depending on the type of animal, size of the pet, and potential damage it might do to the property. Don't necessarily assume that the answer is always no. Even though many landlords have had bad experiences with renters and their pets, you may be able to convince them that you will be the exception.

Moving Abroad

As exciting as it may be to move to another country, it is important to remember that your companion animal may not be regarded or
treated the way it is in the United States. It is essential for you to learn
the habits of the people and the culture of the country you are considering moving to, especially with regard to pets.

Whom Do You Ask?

Here are some suggestions for researching the information you'll
need:

o   Write to the Ministry of Tourism for the country you're consid-
    ering moving to and request information concerning quaran-
    tines, necessary inoculations, and so forth.

o   If your move is because of a job transfer, ask your employer
    (or perhaps Human Resources) what the situation is regarding
    pets in the particular country to which you are being
    transferred.

o   Search on the Internet.

Talk to people who have lived in the country you are considering.

In other words, don't assume; find out. As much as you may want
to take your pet with you, it might not be in its best interest to go. Consider what is best for your pet, and you may find that leaving it behind
with family, friends, or in a new home is a better choice.

Safe Air Travel for Animals

In April 2000, President Bill Clinton signed into law the Safe Air Travel
for Animals Act. This is considered landmark legislation designed to
make air travel safer for pets and other animals. The legislation requires
airlines to provide monthly reports to the U.S. Department of Transpor-
tation Safety on all incidents of loss, injury, or death to animals. These
reports are made available to the public so consumers will be better
informed on specific airlines' track records regarding animal safety.

In addition, the legislation requires improved training in animal
care and safe transport for baggage handlers. So, if you need to travel
by air with your pet, you can now check to see which airlines have the
best safety record for treating companion animals. This should give you
a better sense of security when you are traveling by air and your pet

comes along. The passage of this act reinforces the fact that the public, including legislators, recognizes the special importance of the companion animals in our lives.

If you have ever experienced grief of any kind, you probably learned that it is much easier to bear if you have the support of friends and/or family to share the pain. Often, however, we discover that when we lose a companion animal, our friends and family may not be as comforting as we would hope. In our next chapter, we'll look at ways to enlist the support of friends and family, and even how to reach out to strangers, to seek the comfort you need and desire during the grieving process.

Chapter 10

The Kindness of Strangers

*What we have once enjoyed
we can never lose.
All that we love deeply
becomes a part of us.*

—Helen Keller

Are You Really as Alone as You Feel?

As you may have already discovered, there is not often a lot of societal support when you lose your pet. Well-meaning people might say to you, "I'm sorry." But they are just as likely to say, "It was just a dog, why don't you go to the pound and get another one?" When you hear words like these, you probably want to scream, "You don't understand!"

And, in fact, they don't.

Eileen came to see me two months after her Irish setter, Rusty, died. Rusty had been with Eileen since he was a puppy, and because Eileen was a writer who worked from her home, they had been together all the time. They took several walks every day, and Eileen had liked to call him her "muse" while she was writing. Eileen's husband, Paul, had adored Rusty, too, but he just didn't seem to be grieving as much as she was.

Eileen told me that when she turned to Paul for support, he seemed bewildered that she was "taking it so hard." "After all," Paul said, "even though Rusty was a great dog, he still was only a dog." Eileen couldn't make Paul understand that Rusty had meant much more to her, and that his loss had affected her profoundly. Furthermore, the fact that Paul couldn't seem to understand or share in her grief was making the situation even harder to bear.

Trying to educate well-meaning but misguided folks while you are dealing with your grief is not something you want to do, even if you could. But with a little help and some specific tools, you may be able to enlighten them about the kind of support you need.

This chapter is meant to guide you in helping those people around you who might need some ideas on what to do to support you through this time of grief. Read the chapter, then show it to your loved ones so they can gain some insight on how to help you. It's not that they don't care about you, or don't want to help, they just don't know how. Unless your friends and relatives are bonded to companion animals in the same way you are, providing support for your loss will not be instinctive; they must consciously try to gain understanding. That's what this chapter hopes to provide.

After Your Loss: How to Ask for Help

The following are some suggestions for what you might say to the people around you during your time of grief. Not all of these suggestions will apply, but you will know what you need or want. Don't be afraid to ask others for help. Often, they just need to hear from you specifically what it is that you need. And if the person is not capable of doing what you ask, find someone else who might be more available. Remember they are not trying to hurt you, it's just that they really do not understand. Try not to make yourself feel worse by believing that they are insensitive to your pain or deliberately cruel.

Suggestions for Verbalizing Your Needs

You might give voice to your needs in some of the following ways:

o   I need to talk about my loss. I may frequently need to ask you why it happened to me and to my dear companion. I am struggling with this loss in many ways. Please don't try to fix it; you can't. Just being there will be enough for me.

o   I may need for you to listen again and again about what my loss means to me. Each time I discuss it, it helps me to accept the reality of my pet's death. I may cry; I hope you don't mind. I hope you won't be too uncomfortable, but crying is important to my recovering from this loss.

o   It's okay if you cry, too. In fact, it might make me feel better knowing that you are sympathetic to my feelings, even if you didn't love my pet as I did.

o   I need you to show me that you care for me. Please don't worry if you don't know what to say about my loss. I just need your support and comfort. Don't feel that you are intruding on my life by not calling or leaving me alone. I need companionship even more now. If you can't be with me, please call, send a card, note or e-mail to let me know you're thinking of me. This will help me to know I'm not alone.

o   Please don't tell me how I should feel. All of us are different in our grief, and I am the only one who knows how I feel. Please don't suggest that I should get a new pet right away. I may do that, but it needs to be in my time. If I get a new companion right away, please don't attempt to talk me out of it. It might not be the right decision, but I have to judge that for myself. I promise I won't say later that you should not have let me get a new pet so quickly.

o   Please don't get frustrated with me. I know it's hard for you, but I cannot speed up my grieving process. I can only go at my own pace. I need to meet the grief and accept it, not pretend it isn't there, or try to hide it deep within me. I will never recover from this loss if I do not go through the process of grieving. If you can understand that, you may be able to avoid getting frustrated with me or concerned that my grief will never end. It will.

o   Don't get concerned if I appear to be getting better and then I slip back into grief. It is a normal part of the grieving process to do this. I have learned that waves of grief will come and go, but eventually I will most likely be okay.

o   If I (or perhaps you) can find a pet-loss support group, please go with me. It would mean a lot, as I might not remember everything that was said. It would also be a place where I could share my feelings with others who are going through the same pain. You might help me to get the names of the others in the group, so I will have others to talk to about my grief.

o   Lastly, thank you for being my friend through this time. Thank you for caring, for helping, and for understanding. You are a great blessing, and I will be there for you when and if you ever need me.

Showing Others How to Help

Those of you who try to help another person through the roller coaster of emotions of pet loss are to be commended. It is not easy to help someone move through the stages of grieving, especially if you don't fully understand the process. Knowing what to say or do and what not to say or do is often difficult, at best. We live in a society that doesn't like to talk about death and dying, whether the loved one was a human being or a pet. So, don't be too hard on yourself if you don't understand or relate to your friend or relative's loss. Even if you do understand and relate to the loss, if you find yourself getting angry or frustrated, that's normal,

We don't like to see our friends and loved ones in pain. Often, we think that if we could just come up with the right words or actions, all will be well again. If you have never personally experienced a great loss, it will probably be more difficult to understand, since you have nothing with which to compare it. Don't be afraid to ask for help for yourself from someone who may know more than you do about what a grieving person goes through.

You have many sources for information and advice. The following list should help you find such sources:

o   Veterinarians

o   Pet-loss counselors

o   Pet-loss groups

o   Mental health professionals

o   The Internet

o   Someone you know who has lost a pet

What Not to Say to a Grieving Person

There are certain sayings that often come to mind when we talk about grief. Although they may be true, or you may believe them to be true, they are not always helpful during the time when someone is trying to deal with the thoughts and feelings associated with the loss of a beloved pet. In our attempts to be helpful, we sometimes say things that actually make the grieving person feel worse. The following are some areas and topics you might want to avoid.

o   Don't give advice, pep talks, or talk about your own experiences when trying to help a bereft person. Grieving is a process. There is no time limit on it and your good intentions may be met with anger, hostility, or silence. Try to be patient and understanding, and just listen. If advice is asked for, make sure the person really wants it. You can tell when advice is not wanted. Just listen: Does the person you're advising counter every suggestion you offer with an objection or a reason why it wouldn't work? That's a good sign that advice is not wanted or needed here. A sympathetic ear would be much better received.

o   Don't offer old sayings like, "Time heals all wounds" or "It was God's will." Even though these sayings may be true, grieving people tend to suppress rather than express their grief when they hear these clichés. They often believe that you're right, so they stop talking about what they are feeling. Offering sayings like these will only make their grief last longer.

o   Don't encourage the person to get on with life as if nothing has happened. Grief often slows us down, and we may not have the energy to do what is suggested. Instead, you might want to encourage the person to slow down, and let the grieving process take whatever time is needed.

o   Try not to compare another person's grief (or your own) to the newly bereft. Remember, every human being is different and we process things differently. Comparisons do not help and can cause confusion and frustration for the person who has lost a beloved pet. This is particularly important in pet loss, because there is already very little societal support for the grief felt by pet guardians. Comparing it to another loss probably will be unwelcome and unappreciated.

o   In an effort to be helpful, friends and family may encourage the person to get another pet. In some cases, well-meaning people actually go out and get a pet for the person, thinking that this will help overcome the loss. Please don't do this! Not only will the person feel obligated to keep the new pet, he or she may be deeply offended, feeling that you really don't understand the depth of the attachment to the companion animal. Pets, just like people, are not that easily replaceable. Let the grieving person make the decision about when or if another companion animal is desired.

Activities: How to Elicit the Support You Need

1. Using your journal or tape recorder, make a list of the people from whom you most need and want support. Then make a list of what is most important to you in terms of support for your grief; in other words, quiet listening, companionship, help in finding support groups, etc. This will help you clarify what you need, and who you feel the greatest need to turn to for comfort.

2. Share other parts of your journal or tape with trusted friends and family members, especially the sections you believe best describe your feelings of loss and grief. Seeing or hearing this might make it easier for others to understand the magnitude of your loss, thus making it easier for them to offer support.

If you use some or all of these suggestions, they should be of help to both the person who is grieving and those who are doing their best to be supportive. If you find, however, that you are getting worse and not better, it might be helpful to consult a mental health professional. It's not uncommon to get "stuck" in some phase of the grieving process, but trained professionals can help you get "unstuck." You owe it to yourself and to your companion animal to complete the grieving process so that you can be happy and healthy again.

Peace of Mind and Heart

Many people who have lost their companion animals take great comfort from the following poem. The poem, whose author is unknown, expresses the hope that many pet guardians have: that one day they will be reunited with their cherished friend.

The Rainbow Bridge

Inspired by a Norse legend

By the edge of a woods, at the foot of a hill,
Is a lush green meadow where time stands still.
Where the friends of man and woman do run,
When their time on earth is over and done.

For here, between this world and next,
Is a place where each beloved creature finds rest.
On this golden land, they wait and they play,
'Til the Rainbow Bridge they cross over one day.

No more do they suffer, in pain or in sadness,
For here they are whole, their lives filled with gladness.
Their limbs are restored, their health renewed,
Their bodies have healed, with strength imbued.

They romp through the grass, without even a care
Until one day they start, and sniff the air.
All ears prick forward, eyes dart front to back,
Then all of a sudden, one breaks from the pack.

For just at that instant, their eyes have met;
Together again, both person and pet.
So they run to each other; these friends from long past,
The time of their parting is over at last.

The sadness they felt while they were apart,

Has turned into joy once more in each heart.
They embrace with a love that will last forever,
And then, side by side, they cross over . . . together.

It is a safe assumption that you are reading this book because you or someone you care about has lost a companion animal. In addition to gaining some understanding of what a grieving person experiences, I hope you have also learned that no one has to endure grief alone. Resources exist to help those in need move through the grieving process with the full understanding that what they are feeling is normal, and that their grief will come to an end one day.

You will know when the grieving process is complete because you will have come to the acceptance phase of the experience. No longer will your heart be filled with sadness, pain, and sorrow; instead, you will be able to remember your pet with great love and feel happy that you had the opportunity to experience the friendship of this special being. You will laugh as you remember his or her unique characteristics and antics. Just as no two human beings are alike, no two animals are alike. Your pet was one of a kind and will always be in your heart and soul. You may, at this time, even feel like getting another companion, knowing that you will be able to love again.

At the end of the process, you may want to throw a celebration party. Invite everyone who helped you through your grief. Ask them to bring friends, and expand your circle of people who may need you in the future. In this way, you will be honoring your companion and, at the same time, be giving back what was given to you. Life is a great circle, and death is part of that circle. If we honor life, then honoring death is also appropriate.

Being a pet guardian is a special opportunity, one that creates memories that last a lifetime. Even though we must eventually face the inevitability of our companions' death, the joy they bring us in life helps to soften the sorrow we feel when they die. Always remember that grief is temporary, but the precious and joyful memories of the time you shared with your companion will last forever. With each life that we encounter, we have one more chance to celebrate the uniqueness of all living beings.

Suggested Reading

Anderson, M. 1994. *Coping with Sorrow on the Loss of Your Pet*. Los Angeles: Peregrine Press.

Bloom-Feshback, J., and S. Bloom-Feshbach. 1987. *The Psychology of Separation and Loss*. San Francisco: Jossey-Bass Publications.

Bogard, G. .2000. How to Cope with the Death of a Pet. Tomball Veterinary Clinic. Retrieved from the Internet 10-20-2001 http://www:thevet.com

Bowlby, J. 1969. *Attachment and Loss*, vol .1. New York: Basic Books.

Caras, R. A. 1997. *The Bond*. New York: Simon & Schuster.

Colgrove, M., H. H. Bloomfield, and P. McWilliams. 1991. *Surviving, Healing and Growing*. Los Angeles: Prelude Press.

Colleague Assistance and Support Program (CLASP). 2001. *California Psychologist* 34(11):20-21.

Downing, R. 2000. *Pets Living with Cancer*. Lakewood, CO: AAHA Press.

Engel, J. 1989. Elderpet strengthens bond between companion animals and elderly people. *People, Animals and Environment* Spring Delta Society: Renton, WA.

Friedman, E., A. H. Katcher, J. J. Lynch, and S. A. Thomas. 1980. Animal Companions and One-Year Survival of Patients After Discharge from a Coronary Care Unit. *Public Health Reports*: July-August 4:307-312.

Friedman, E., A. H. Katcher, S. A. Thomas, J. J. Lynch, and D. Messent. 1983. Social interaction and blood pressure. *Journal of Nervous and Mental Disease* 17(8):461-465.

Friedman, M. 2001. *Post Traumatic Stress Disorder: The Latest Assessment and Treatment Strategies*. Kansas City, MO: Dean Psychological Press Corporation.

Greene, L. A. 2001. It's only a dog: the psychologists' role in the pet bereavement process. *The California Psychologist* May/June 34(6).

Greene, L. A., and W. Sife. 1998. Classification of Pet Owners. *Newsletter of the Association for Pet Loss and Bereavement Counselors.* Winter 1(4).

Henderson, N. G. 2001. Who will care for your pets when you no longer can? *The Companion* Winter 13(4). Santa Fe, CA: Helen Woodward Animal Center Rancho, p. 5.

International Critical Incident Stress Foundation. 1996. Critical Incident Stress Information Sheet. Retrieved from the Internet 1-20-2002. http://home.earthlink.net/hopefull/debriefi.htm

Kale, M. 1992. Who's Got that bonded feeling? *Interactions* 10(2):5.

Lagoni, L., C. Butler, and S. Hetts. 1994. *The Human-Animal Bond and Grief*. Philadelphia: W. B. Saunders & Company.

Lerner, H. 1985. *The Dance of Anger*. New York: HarperCollins.

Medura, L. 1986. Pet Cemeteries. *Animals* July/August, p. 9.

Meichenbaum, D. 1985. *Stress Inoculation Training*. New York: Pergamon Press.

Milani, M. 1998. *Preparing for the Loss of Your Pet*. Rocklin, CA: Prima Publishing.

Montagu, A. 1971. *Touching*. New York: Columbia University Press.

Montgomery, M., and H. Montgomery. 2000. *I Remember: A Book About My Special Pet*. Minneapolis, MN: Montgomery Press.

———. 1993. *A Final Act of Caring*. Minneapolis, MN: Montgomery Press

Nieburg, H., and A. Fischer. 1982. *Pet Loss: A Thoughtful Guide for Adults and Children*. New York: Harper & Row

Prigerson, H. G., and S. C. Jacobs. 2001. Caring for bereaved patients: All the doctors just suddenly go. *JAMA* 286(11).

Robin, M. 1990. *Pets and the Socialization of Children*. Minneapolis, MN: University of Minnesota Press.

Serpall, J. 1986. *In the Company of Animals*. New York: Basil Blackwell Ltd.

Sibbitt, S. 1991. *Oh Where Has My Pet Gone?* A Pet Loss Memory Book: Ages 3–103. Wayzata, MN: B. Libby Press.

Sife, W. 1998. *The Loss of a Pet*. New York: Howell Book House.

State Humane Association of California. 2000. *California Animal Laws Handbook*. Pacific Grove, CA: State Humane Association of California.

Stewart, C. S., J. C. Thrush, G. S. Paulus, and P. Hafner. 1985. The elderly's adjustment to the loss of a companion animal: People-pet dependency. *Death Studies* 9:383-393.

Tousley, M. 2000. Thinking It Through: Exploring Questions About Euthanasia. Retrieved from the Internet 10-20-2001. http://www:griefhealing.com

Tousley, M. 2000. Loss and the Burden of Guilt. Retrieved from the Internet No date. http://www griefhealing.com

van der Kolk, B. A., McFarlane, A., and L. Weisaeth, eds. 1996. *Traumatic Stress: The Effects of Overwhelming Experience on Mind, Body and Society*. New York: Guilford Press.

Walkowicz, C. 1985. What if your pet outlives you? Plan now for its physical and financial security. *Dog Fancy* July.

White, B. 1993. *Pet Love*. New York: William Morrow & Co.

Williams, T. 1987. *Post Traumatic Stress Disorders: A Handbook for Clinicians*. Cincinnati, OH: Disabled American Veterans National Headquarters.

Resources

General Resources

The Animal Medical Center, New York
(212) 838-8100
Support groups and counselor referrals for the New York City area

The Delta Society
(800) 869-6898
This organization publishes a Nationwide Pet Bereavement Directory

University of California, Davis, School of Veterinary Medicine
(800) 565-1526
Pet-Loss Support Hotline

Grief Support and Pet Loss Resources

Association for Pet Loss and Bereavement
www.aplb.org

The Delta Society
http://www.deltasociety.org/dsn300.htm

The Humane Society of the United States
http://www.hsus.org

Purdue University School of Veterinary Medicine
http://www.vet.purdue.edu

University of California, Davis, Veterinary School of Medicine
http://www.vetnet.ucdavis.edu/petloss/index.htm

Helpful Websites

American Veterinary Medical Association
www.avma.org/care4pets/lossandi.htm

Our Pals
http://216.149.169.246

www.griefhealing.com

www.creatures.com

www.dogshavesouls.com

www.superdog.com/petloss.htm

www.petloss.com

Hospice Information

Nikki Hospice Foundation for Pets
www.csum.edu/pethospice

Pet Memorials, Tributes, Keepsakes

http://thunder/prohosting.com/~easyshop

www.theurnist.com

www.in-memory-of-pets.com

www.foreverpets.com

www.petgarden.com

www.animalnews.com/memorial

www.kent.net/eggcellent

Recommended Reading for Adults

Anderson, M. 1996. *Coping with Sorrow on the Loss of Your Pet*, 2d ed., Los AngelesPeregrine Press.

Bowlby, J. 2000. *Attachment*, 2d ed. New York: Basic Books.

———. 1990. *A Secure Base: Parent-Child Attachment and Healthy Human Development*. New York: Basic Books.

Kubler-Ross, E. 1969. *On Death and Dying*. Collier Books/Macmillan Publishing.

———. 1975. *Death: The Final Stage of Growth*. New York: Prentice-Hall.

Milani, M. 1998. *Preparing for the Loss of Your Pet: Saying Goodbye with Love, Dignity, and Peace of Mind*. Rocklin, CA: Prima Publishing.

Montgomery, M., and H. Montgomery. 1993. *A Final Act of Caring: Ending the Life of an Animal Friend*. Minneapolis, MN: Montgomery Press.

———. 1991. *Good-Bye My Friend: Grieving the Loss of a Pet*. Minneapolis, MN: Montgomery Press.

Mooney, S. 1983. *A Snowflake in My Hand*. Audioscope. New York: Delacourt Press.

Nieberg, H. A., and A. Fischer. 1996. *Pet Loss: A Thoughtful Guide for Adults & Children*. New York: HarperPerennial Library.

Quintana, M. L., S. L. Veleba, and H. King. 1998. *It's Okay to Cry*. Perrysburg, OH: K & K Communications.

Sife, W. 1998. *The Loss of a Pet*, New revised and expanded ed. New York: Howell Book House.

Recommended Reading for Children

Sibbitt, S. 1991. *Oh Where Has My Pet Gone? A Pet Loss Memory Book, Ages 3–103*. Wayzata, MN: B. Libby Press.

Viorst, J. 1971. *The Tenth Good Thing About Barney*. New York: Athenum.

White, E. B. 1952. *Charlotte's Web*. New York: Harper Junior.

References

Albom, M. 1997. *Tuesdays with Morrie, an Old Man, a Young Man, and Life's Greatest Lesson.* New York: Doubleday.

American Veterinary Medical Association. 2001. *Guidelines for Veterinary Hospice Care.* Schaumburg, IL: American Veterinary Medical Association.

Anderson, W. P., P. Warwick, C. M. Reid, and G. J. Jennings. 1992. Pet ownership and risk factors for cardiovascular disease. *Medical Journal of Australia* 157:298-301.

Beauchamp, L. 2000. Euthanasia: Background. Microsoft Encarta Online Encyclopedia. Retrieved from the Internet 12-11-2001. http://encarta.msm.com/find/print.asp?&pg#8.

Beck, A. M., and A. H. Katcher. 1996. *Between Pets and People.* West Lafayette, IN: Purdue University Press.

California Animal Laws Handbook. 2000. Pacific Grove, CA: State Humane Assoc. of California.

Caras, R. A. 1997. *The Bond.* New York: Simon & Schuster.

Center for Information Management. 1997. *U.S. Pet Ownership and Demographic Sourcebook.* Schaumburg, IL: American Veterinary Medical Association.

Ellis, A. 1985. *Clinical Applications of Rational Emotive Therapy.* New York: Plenum Publishing.

Friedman, E., A. H. Katcher, J. J. Lynch, and S. A. Thomas. 1980. Animal companions and one-year survival of patients after discharge from a coronary care unit. *Public Health Reports* 4:307–312.

Horney, K. 1950. *Neurosis and Human Growth: The Struggle Toward Self-Realization.* New York: Norton Publishing.

Hospice of the North Coast. *Volunteer Manual.* Encinitas, CA.

Johnson, S. A., and A. Aamodt. 1985. *Wolf Pack: Tracking Wolves in the Wild.* Minneapolis, MN: Lerner Publications.

Kubler-Ross, E. 1969. *On Death and Dying.* New York: Macmillan.

Lachman, L. 2000. Out of the Doghouse and onto the Couch. *Psychology Today* 7(3), May/June, p. 7.

Leary, T. 1983. *Flashbacks: An Autobiography.* Boston: Houghton-Mifflin.

Lockwood, R., and F. Ascione, eds. 1997. *Cruelty to Animals and Interpersonal Violence: Readings in Research and Applications.* West Lafayette, IN: Purdue University Press.

Morris, H. 1971. *Guilt and Shame.* Belmont, CA: Wadsworth Publishing Co.

Nicholson, J., S. Kemp-Wheeler, and D. Griffiths. 1995. Distress arising from the end of a guide dog partnership. *Anthrozoos* 8(2):100-109.

San Diego Union Tribune. 2000. Orangutan Ken Allen Is Put to Sleep at San Diego Zoo. December 2, 2000, p. B1.

Saunders, D. C. 1990. *Hospice of North Coast Volunteer Manual.* Encinitas, CA: Hospice of North Coast.

Squire, A. 2000. *Why Do Pets Do That?* New York: Globe Digests.

Survivors of Suicide San Diego (S.O.S.). 1992. *After My Loss.* La Mesa, CA: Harbor House West Publishers.

Twain, M. 1924. *The Autobiography of Mark Twain.* New York. Harper & Brothers.

Westendorf, J. 1996. *Historical Look at Euthanasia.* Paper presented at Christian Life Resources National Convention at the Wisconsin Lutheran Seminary, Mequon, Wisconsin. Retrieved from the Internet 12-10-2001. http://www.christianlifesources.com

Wolman, B. B. 1982. *Handbook of Developmental Psychology.* Englewood Cliffs, New Jersey: Prentice Hall.

Lorri A. Greene, Ph.D., is a licensed clinical psychologist who has been helping people grieve the loss of their pets for more than twenty years. In 1986, Greene cofounded the San Diego County Pet Bereavement Program, one of the few programs in the United States offering continuous support for those who have lost companion animals. Dr. Greene conducts frequent pet-loss support groups, and she speaks nationally and internationally on the topic of pet loss and the human-animal bond. She maintains a private practice in San Diego, California.

Jacquelyn Landis is a freelance writer and author of *The Insiders' Guide to San Diego,* as well as numerous other books and articles about life in San Diego. She lives with her cat, Kali, in the San Diego area.

Foreword writer **Alan M. Beck, Sc.D.,** is one of the nation's leading experts on the human-animal bond. He coauthored *Between Pets and People: The Importance of Animal Companionship.* Beck is professor of animal ecology and director of the Center for the Human-Animal Bond, School of Veterinary Medicine, Purdue University.

Some Other
New Harbinger Titles

The Stop Walking on Eggshells Workbook, Item SWEW $18.95

Conquer Your Critical Inner Voice, Item CYIC $15.95

The PTSD Workbook, Item PWK $17.95

Hypnotize Yourself Out of Pain Now!, Item HYOP $14.95

The Depression Workbook, 2nd edition, Item DWR2 $19.95

Beating the Senior Blues, Item YCBS $17.95

Shared Confinement, Item SDCF $15.95

Handbook of Clinical Psychopharmacology for Therpists, 3rd edition, Item HCP3 $55.95

Getting Your Life Back Together When You Have Schizophrenia Item GYLB $14.95

Do-It-Yourself Eye Movement Technique for Emotional Healing, Item DIYE $13.95

Stop the Anger Now, Item SAGN $17.95

The Self-Esteem Workbook, Item SEWB $18.95

The Habit Change Workbook, Item HBCW $19.95

The Memory Workbook, Item MMWB $18.95

The Anxiety & Phobia Workbook, 3rd edition, Item PHO3 $19.95

Beyond Anxiety & Phobia, Item BYAP $19.95

Stop Walking on Eggshells, Item WOE $15.95

The Healing Sorrow Workbook, Item HSW $17.95

The Relaxation & Stress Reduction Workbook, 5th edition, Item RS5 $19.95

Stop Controlling Me!, Item SCM $13.95

The Anger Control Workbook, Item ACWB $17.95

Call **toll free, 1-800-748-6273,** or log on to our online bookstore at **www.newharbinger.com** to order. Have your Visa or Mastercard number ready. Or send a check for the titles you want to New Harbinger Publications, Inc., 5674 Shattuck Ave., Oakland, CA 94609. Include $4.50 for the first book and 75¢ for each additional book, to cover shipping and handling. (California residents please include appropriate sales tax.) Allow two to five weeks for delivery.

Prices subject to change without notice.